CHRISTIAN COUNSELING SERVICES
N Ph.D.
STREET
45701

Assertion Training

Sherwin B. Cotler & Julio J. Guerra
Assertion Training

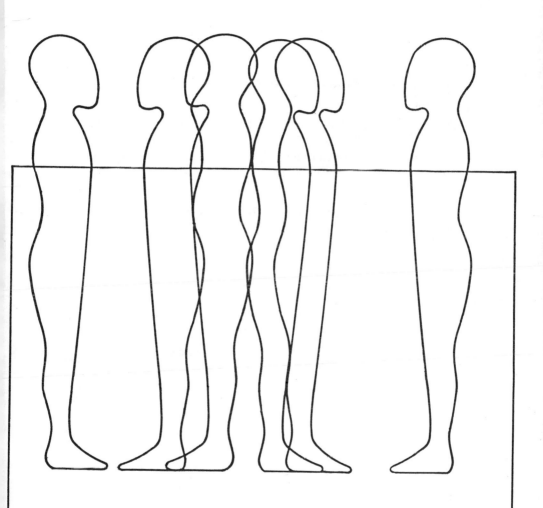

A Humanistic-Behavioral Guide to Self-Dignity

Research Press   2612 North Mattis Avenue   Champaign, Illinois 61820

To my parents, Leo and Bessie Cotler
for the love, understanding, and support
they have given me throughout my life

In memory of my father, Julio J. Guerra, M.D.
—a man who taught me "where it is at"

Pronouns cause authors and editors a good deal of concern, especially today with the recognition that many books and articles appear to be "sexist" by referring to all individuals using the male gender. In writing the draft of this book, we used "he/she" and "she/he" pronouns in equal numbers throughout the text. However this became very confusing at times. Consequently, upon the editor's request, we have referred to most therapists, clients, and others in this book by using masculine pronouns. The reason for this change is strictly for smoother reading, and it is in no way intended to show a preference for one sex over the other.

Contents

Foreword

I recently had the opportunity of viewing a videotape which was made a few years ago of Julio and Sherwin lecturing on assertion training. Although some of the basic concepts have remained the same, I was astonished by the amount of depth that has been added since that time.

When Sherwin and Julio were first developing their approach to teaching assertive skills, procedures such as how to defend oneself from criticism seemed very clear cut, behavioristic, and almost mechanical. It seemed to me that for almost any response there was an automatic set of rules to follow. Several basic approach and protective skills were developed, but somehow this wasn't sufficient.

Through several years of running workshops and treatment groups with Sherwin and Julio, we have begun to incorporate many ideas that were typically not attended to previously. Changing feelings about oneself certainly occurred through social skill training; however, dealing with these feelings directly has been added to the repertoire. This is sometimes done through the use of Gestalt techniques, through the exploration of body image, nonverbal communication, and so forth. Working with emotions as well as behaviors seems to be an important asset of assertion training which, rightfully, deserves considerable attention. Assertion training deals with developing and maintaining a set of values. For some people, assertion training means being successful at keeping people at a distance. For us, it primarily means developing social skills to draw people closer to one another within an honest relationship. As sophisticated as we think we are, basically we still need support and comfort from one another. Occasionally a protective skill may be used, but in most cases a relationship can be maintained and enhanced through an honest, clear communication. Learning to get closer to others is of primary importance not only on an individual basis, but in larger groups of people as well. Assertion training can be one way to help people attain some skills and comfort in reaching out to others.

All of us have, at one time or another, been in situations where we have been nonassertive. My nonassertive behaviors were not atypical. I had problems saying "No," because I didn't want to risk the loss of another person's approval. Therefore, I was often busy doing things I had little interest in, and yet I did not want to risk the possible consequences of honesty. I also had difficulty in expressing my anger, sadness, or hurt. I had been told in many ways while growing up that those emotions were not for sharing. This created distance in my relationships that I really did not want to have, but I didn't know how to change.

Assertion training has helped me focus on who I am and what I want in relationships. This certainly did not occur overnight or without any problems. Sometimes I would be aggressive rather than assertive, other times I would be indirect rather than direct. It looked so easy, but it really wasn't. My anxiety would rise in new situations, and that in itself was uncomfortable. Over the past two years I have seen definite changes in the way I interact with others. I now feel closer, more alive, and less restrained in my relationships. My feelings about myself have also been altered. I feel more assured of myself and less threatened by others. I also feel that I have developed a sensitivity towards others that had been masked for years while I was desperately trying to protect myself.

I do not consider myself particularly unusual. I think that many people, like myself, are programmed to be nonassertive. Family values and our culture put an emphasis on such things as not getting angry, not talking back, being quiet, and respecting elders. We are told that honesty is not always the best policy, because honesty may include exposing our own sensitivity. So we find ourselves becoming more and more isolated. What a shame!

Assertion training is very much in vogue now. It can be an enhancement for people who are already functioning adequately as well as for those who have more severe problems. However, I feel that we will see special interest groups utilize assertion training in the future. These groups will be comprised primarily of women and children. The feminist movement has elicited an awareness to the changing value system of women. No longer will as many women remain dutifully quiet or socially isolated within the family unit. However, some skill training and anxiety reduction may be helpful for them before embarking on these new pursuits.

Children, on the other hand, do not have the freedom some people think they have. If a child is assertive, this may involve questioning authority and most adults would balk at this. So I feel that we will have to delve into the child's world of adult authorities and give support and training to the adults as well as to the children.

All of this seems very exciting to me, but the adaptations of what we now know as assertion training also seem a little mystifying. As much as assertion training has evolved over the past five years, it will probably continue to change in the future when focusing on special people with individual needs. It is with excitement that I look forward to the prospects to come.

Susan Morgan Cotler, M.A.
California State University, Long Beach

Acknowledgments

We would like to express our special appreciation to those who have contributed in some way to the writing of this book. To begin with, we would like to thank William Seefeldt for his critical review of our manuscript and for the many insightful suggestions he has made throughout our association together. To Zev Wanderer at the Center for Behavior Therapy in Beverly Hills, California and Manuel Smith at the Veterans Hospital in Sepulveda, California, we are indebted for much of the knowledge we gained during our internship years. To John Flowers and Susan Morgan Cotler we are grateful not only for what they have added to our warehouse of assertive knowledge, but also for their friendship and understanding. In terms of meeting deadlines and deciphering our coded handwriting, we might still be working on this book if it were not for the typing skills of Jean Lamb and Margaret Connole.

Finally, we would like to acknowledge all of those individuals who have participated in our assertion training workshops and groups. These are the people who have really made our work enjoyable and who have motivated us to write about our assertion training philosophy and procedures. Perhaps unknowingly, these individuals have added something very special to our own personal lives. To each and every one of you, we would like to express our appreciation and thanks.

Part 1 Establishing
the foundation

1 Introduction

Rationale for assertiveness: Self-respect

This book is about assertion training and, more specifically, about the assertion training we have been doing since 1970. The intent of the book is to give you an understanding of what is meant by "assertive behaviors" and how one goes about teaching these assertive behaviors to others. For the most part, this is a how-to book in that we have attempted to present our training procedures so that others can clearly see what we do in our assertion training groups. However, we have also described our rationale for using these various procedures so that you can understand why specific procedures are utilized at certain times and not at others. In addition, we have attempted to convey our philosophy of human worth; a philosophy which emphasizes the uniqueness and importance of every individual and the individual's need to maintain his dignity and self-respect.

Assertion training is primarily concerned with two major interpersonal goals—anxiety reduction and social skill training. Behaviorally speaking, an individual who is assertive can establish close, interpersonal relationships; can protect himself from being taken advantage of by others; can make decisions and free choices in life; can recognize and acquire more of his interpersonal needs; and can verbally and non-verbally express a wide range of feelings and thoughts, both positive and negative. This is to be accomplished without experiencing undue amounts of anxiety or guilt and without violating the rights and dignity of others in the process. In addition to reducing anxiety and guilt so that previously learned behaviors can be carried out more effectively, assertion training attempts to teach new verbal and nonverbal

3

communication skills that were previously lacking in the individual's repertoire.

One of the major goals of assertion training is to support the individual's recognition of himself as an important living being who is entitled to his thoughts, emotions, and feelings which need not be negotiated away to others with the resulting loss of self-respect or dignity. Although assertion training has been discussed and researched primarily by behavioral therapists, its underlying philosophy is also very consistent with a humanistic orientation. Assertiveness involves the recognition and expression of an individual's wants, values, needs, expectations, dislikes, and desires. As such, this not only involves getting in better touch with yourself, but also affects how you interact with other human beings.

To begin with, we believe that you must not only know yourself in terms of likes and dislikes, needs and desires, strengths and weaknesses, but also that you must learn to like and feel comfortable with yourself. Before you can expect to nourish others, you must first understand and take care of yourself. The most important thing in your life is *you*—only if you respect and take care of yourself will you be able to be of ongoing help to others.

This is not to say that the attitude "by helping others, you help yourself" is incorrect. However, if you constantly live your life only for your children, your spouse, or your boss and without reference to yourself and your own needs, you will eventually begin to feel bitter and resentful. As a result, you may begin to avoid these people and might even terminate these relationships. There is absolutely nothing wrong with helping others—as long as it does not repeatedly interfere with your own needs, self-respect, or dignity. At the very foundation of assertion training and the humanistic philosophy can be found a recognition of the value of human worth and the unique nature of each human being. Each of us has an individual value system and the right to believe in and desire certain things. We may not always get what we desire, but we still have the right to want, especially when these wants do not interfere with the safety or self-respect of others.

To express one's desires and values without infringing upon the rights of others is a basic step in learning to be assertive. We can conceive of no social interaction where one person should be the underdog or scapegoat for another person. We strongly endorse the equality of all human beings—the equality of women with men, of children with adults, of employees with employers, of customers with business people, of aged with youth. We cannot conceive of an interaction where one individual should have to negotiate away or lose his dignity as a person.

As Glasser (1965) has indicated, there is the need to feel worthwhile, the need to care for and love others, and the need to be cared for and loved by others. We understand that in order for us to have our own needs filled in a relationship, we must be prepared to fill the needs of others as well. However, this can be done without losing sight of the fact that our own needs and values are also important and should not be sacrificed in the process. In assertion training, we have frequently encountered individuals who do not exercise the option of saying "No" or "Yes" or "I want." Our experience with these individuals has been that, although they are smiling and giving on the exterior, inside they can be very angry and resentful of the fact that they are always giving and seldom receiving. As a result, it is often difficult for these individuals to achieve a lasting and meaningful relationship with other people.

Once the individual is able to recognize, feel comfortable with, and satisfy some of his own personal needs, then it is much easier and more enjoyable for him to respond to the needs and values of others. He can then truly give more of himself and feel better in the process of nourishing others. For those individuals who are basically assertive, taking care of oneself and the nourishing of others occur simultaneously. However, for those who have not learned to love and respect themselves, this is the first order of business.

Occasions for assertive behavior

Reducing interpersonal anxiety, promoting more open and successful communication, expressing positive feelings of love and appreciation, enhancing feelings of self-respect and dignity in confrontations with others—these are some of the situations where assertive behaviors are appropriate. Whether it involves meeting and establishing a relationship with someone you do not know very well, expressing an annoyance to a good friend, or disarming anger and sorting issues with a fellow employee, we believe that an individual who is assertive will be able to handle the situation more successfully. It is recognized that the assertive individual may not be successful or satisfy his needs in every situation that he acts assertively, or even that he will respond assertively on each and every occasion that he has the opportunity to do so. However, by knowing how to respond assertively and by choosing to do so in certain situations, the individual will be able to satisfy more of his needs than by making no response or responding in a nonassertive or aggressive manner.

In some situations, the individual may know how to respond assertively and deliberately choose not to do so if he feels that the consequences of his assertiveness will be too punitive. For example, an individual may not ask his boss for a raise if he feels that this request will more than likely result in the loss of his job which he needs to keep at this time. On the other hand, he may choose to take the risk of losing a job, dissolving a marriage, or alienating a friend if he feels that to maintain the relationship will result in a significant loss of self-respect or dignity. Consequently, the individual must not only know how to apply assertive behaviors in real-life situations, he must be able to evaluate the situation and discriminate as to when assertive behaviors will yield punitive consequences as well as benefits.

The assertion trainer

Before you begin to train others (especially if you are doing this for a fee or are working with individuals who are nonassertive or aggressive over a wide range of situations), you should be basically assertive yourself. All of the cognitive understanding you have of the literature on this topic will be of only limited value in actively working with others in a systematic fashion unless you are able to carry out most of these behaviors yourself. This means having skills not only in ways of protecting yourself so that you are not "victimized" by others, but also having skills in establishing and maintaining positive, meaningful, and ongoing relationships with a wide variety of other people.

For those of you who are already basically assertive in your daily lives, an understanding of fundamental learning theory principles (e.g., Wolpe, 1958, 1969; Ullmann & Krasner, 1965; Honig, 1966; Reynolds, 1968; Bandura, 1969; Franks, 1969; Kanfer & Phillips, 1970) and of the assertion literature (e.g., Salter, 1949; Wolpe, 1958, 1969; Wolpe & Lazarus, 1966; Lazarus, 1968; Fensterheim, 1972; Alberti & Emmons, 1970, 1974; Phelps & Austin, 1975) will be extremely valuable. Although these references on learning theory and assertion training are in no way complete, they do comprise some of the more basic sources.

In addition, some firsthand training, an apprenticeship, or, at the very least, the observation of others doing assertion training will, in our opinion, prove to be extremely helpful in embarking upon the training of others. One of our major concerns in conducting our two- or four-day workshops on assertion training is that we sometimes see individuals who, as a result of participating in one workshop, consider themselves "experts" in this field, and, with no additional training, begin to teach courses or run groups in assertion training. Needless to say, we feel this is a rather presumptuous action. This is not to say that a therapist should avoid trying out some of the ideas obtained in a workshop, but rather that he should be cautious as to how his expertise is advertised until a sufficient amount of training is obtained.

We urge the people we train in workshops to run their first assertion training group or individual sessions with as many co-trainers as possible. The intra-group peer supervision can be a useful safeguard from the problems that result from inadequate experience. It also serves to relieve much of the initial anxiety of trying something different.

In a recent survey of participants who had attended one of our assertion training workshops, eighty-seven percent of the respondents indicated that they had derived some personal gain, in terms of their own assertive behavior, as a result of participating in the workshop. Hopefully, this will be the *beginning* for many of them in becoming more effective assertion trainers in their own right.

We have written this manual primarily for those who work with others in a therapeutic, teaching, or training capacity. As such, we have attempted to present the material in a systematic manner which can be used to assist others in achieving more of their assertive goals and feeling better about themselves in the process. In addition, we believe this book will be helpful to those individuals who feel a need to improve their own assertive skills and who are looking for some direction to take in order to achieve this aim. The book is not intended as a substitute for some training or therapy when, in fact, this may be called for; nor is it a replacement for some further in-depth study of the assertion literature. The material presented in this manual is primarily intended as an introduction to the practical issues in assertion training *and* as a useful handbook for the therapist conducting assertion training. Using this manual as a complement to some in-service training and the further study of theoretical issues will, hopefully, help assure the depth and effectiveness of your assertion training.

2 Assertive vignettes

This chapter describes some typical situations in which assertive behaviors may be appropriate. In conducting workshops for professionals who will be teaching assertive behaviors to others, we frequently begin the workshop by having the participants role-play a number of these situations. The various situations or "vignettes of assertiveness" can be divided into four separate categories. One dimension reflects the intimacy of the interaction; that is, whether the interaction is taking place with a stranger or a situational relationship versus an interaction with a friend or intimate relationship. Interactions where you hardly know the other individual or where the relationship will cease after some business has been transacted—smiling and saying hello to someone you pass on the street, talking with the garage mechanic about fixing your car—fall into the first category; whereas an interaction with a close friend, lover, boss, or spouse would fall into the second category. A second dimension involves whether the individual is making a social approach or a request response versus a situation where the individual is protecting himself or refusing something in the interaction. For example, requesting more physical contact from your spouse would fit into one category and defending yourself against slanderous name-calling would fit into the other category.

As indicated in Table 1, the four dimensions can be represented by a 2x2 matrix with the following categories: Social approach or request responses with strangers and situational relationships, social approach or request responses with friends and intimate relationships, protective or refusal responses with strangers and situational relationships, and

9

Table 1   *Interaction between assertive responses and different relationship levels*

	Social approach or request responses	Protective or refusal responses
Strangers and situational relationships		
Friends and intimate relationships		

protective or refusal responses with friends and intimate relationships.

It has been our experience that most assertion situations fall into one of these four categories, and that clients frequently experience the majority of their assertion difficulties in some categories but not others. For some individuals, it may be relatively easy to refuse a request from a stranger, yet it may be very difficult to refuse a friend a loan of $10. For another person, being able to refuse both close friends and strangers may be much easier than to ask someone for a date. Our experience has been that everyone has at least some difficulty in one of these four areas at one time or another. That is, no one is assertive one hundred percent of the time—at least no one that we have met thus far. Whereas some individuals can act assertively a good deal of the time across

10

these four categories and, consequently, feel pretty good about themselves in terms of their assertive behaviors, others experience a great deal of difficulty. The latter individuals are prime candidates for some assertion training.

Alberti & Emmons (1974) have described a somewhat similar classification scheme in differentiating between the *situational* nonassertive/aggressive individual and the *generalized* nonassertive/aggressive individual. Whereas the *situational* individual may respond in a nonassertive or an aggressive manner in specific situations or with specific individuals, the *generalized* individual *typically* responds in this manner over a wide variety of situations and with a greater number of people. As Alberti & Emmons (1974) have indicated, the *situational* nonassertive/aggressive individual can be a relatively healthy person who, with or without professional help, may learn to successfully initiate more assertive behaviors. The *generalized* nonassertive/aggressive individual, however, will probably require some form of professional attention in order to overcome these behavioral deficits.

The following vignettes are grouped according to the four categories of assertion described in Table 1. As you read through these situations, we would like you to visualize yourself in this situation, visualize handling the situation in what you feel is an appropriate assertive manner, and decide if you are experiencing high or low levels of anxiety in this visualization process.

Social approach or request responses
with strangers and situational relationships

Eye contact
Visualize that you are beginning to talk with someone of the opposite sex who you do not know very well. You are standing at a comfortable distance from the other person and you are looking directly at the person's eyes as you begin to talk. Go ahead now and visualize that scene.

Now visualize that same scene again only this time visualize yourself smiling, if you did not do so before, or visualize yourself keeping a straight face if you were smiling in the first scene.

11

This may appear to be a rather innocuous scene; however, the fact of the matter is that many people have a good deal of trouble in maintaining satisfactory eye contact when they are talking. This can be interpreted to mean that the person is nervous, shy, uncertain of himself, or, generally, nonassertive. Because eye contact is one of the first and most basic interactions that an individual has with another person, it is one of the first assertive approach behaviors that we teach. Good eye contact, like other assertive behaviors, is a learned skill.

Self-praise
Think of four positive qualities you have. Now visualize yourself describing these qualities to someone else who you are just meeting for the first time.

Almost everyone has, at the very least, four positive characteristics. However, some individuals experience a great deal of difficulty in identifying any good things about themselves: They are more accustomed to thinking of themselves in negative terms. Others can think of positive qualities but have difficulty relating these to other people. One of our goals in assertion training is for the individual to be able to acknowledge personal positive qualities, both to himself and to others. In order to be a good friend to others, you first must be a good friend to yourself. In part, this includes your ability to praise yourself rather than always describing yourself in negative terms. If you do not take care of and respect yourself, no one else will.

Did you know how to word your self-praise? Is your anxiety very high?

Introducing yourself
You are in a group meeting where most people do not know one another. You are sitting in your chair and the leader of the group asks each of you to tell the others what you do for a living and to describe some of your hobbies. Visualize that scene.

Now visualize that you are asked to do the same thing, only this time you are asked to stand and come to the front of the room before making your introduction. As you visual-

12

ize this scene, imagine that the person one seat away from you is walking toward the front of the room and that it will soon be your turn. Then imagine that this person finishes with his introduction and it is now your turn to stand up, go to the front of the room, and address the audience.

Did you feel more anxious when the other person was introducing himself or when you were standing in front of the room? Were you able to remember what your hobbies are, or did your mind go blank at first? This exercise is closely related to the previous scene of self-praise. Some people will do practically anything to avoid attention, and when attention is focused on them, their anxiety skyrockets. Also, the anticipatory anxiety that individuals sometimes experience is often greater than the anxiety in the actual situation. Another goal of assertion training is to teach the individual how to handle and successfully reduce anxiety.

Conversations

You are at a party and there are several people present whom you have never met before. You notice one person to whom you are attracted, and you decide you would like to get to know this person better. You walk over to the individual, introduce yourself and begin talking. Visualize yourself in this situation and picture what happens.

Decide if you knew how to start the conversation and reflect on how anxious you were in visualizing this scene.

Now visualize that the person you are interested in meeting is standing and talking with a small group of other people. Your task is now to visualize yourself walking over to this group and becoming a part of their conversation so that you can get to know the person better.

Now imagine that you are talking with someone at this party when you notice an old friend come in whom you have not seen for a long time. You want to terminate your present conversation and go over and see your old friend. Imagine yourself terminating the conversation and going over to meet your friend.

Starting, maintaining, and terminating conversations are some of the most basic assertive skills. Conversation skills are also some of the skills most requested by members in asser-

13

tion training groups. This is not surprising because individuals who are either nonassertive or aggressive are often isolated from others. Since learning how to talk and interact with others can help to reduce this isolation, it is crucial that conversation training be a part of the assertion training process.

In the restaurant

Visualize that you are in a fancy restaurant and have ordered a steak cooked the way you like it best. However, when the steak is brought to your table, it is not cooked the way you ordered it. You therefore refuse the steak and request to have it cooked the way you originally asked.

Did you know how to assertively refuse the improperly prepared steak and request something different? Is your anxiety very high at this point?

Even though the meal is quite expensive, some individuals would rather go ahead and eat the steak than "cause a scene" and have it returned. The person will often rationalize and make excuses: "Oh well, they cooked it right the last time I was here," "Since I am not paying for the meal, I'll just keep quiet," "I just will not come back here anymore." It is important that we learn how to get needs met instead of making up excuses. This is one example where someone is paying for services; consequently, there is no reason why the individual should accept something less than what was requested and is being paid for.

The garage

You have taken your car in for repairs and have come to pick it up the next day. The service manager now informs you that your car is not ready, even though he agreed to call you yesterday if your car would not be ready by today. Since your car is not ready and a friend dropped you off and did not wait, you are requesting the use of a loan car, some taxi money, or a ride so that you can get across town to work. The service manager is giving you a bad time, and you cannot wait the hour and a half until he says the car will be ready. Visualize how you would handle the situation.

14

Did you know how to keep your point clear in the conversation as the service manager made excuses? Did you become angry and verbally abusive to the service manager? Did your anxiety begin to shoot upward?

We feel that part of assertiveness involves being able to stay with a situation and maintain a reasonably low level of anxiety when someone is giving you a bad time or trying to take advantage of you. In the previous example, the customer is well within his rights to ask for some transportation to work in that the service manager had agreed to call the customer if the car was not ready on time. Even when this agreement was broken, some customers would not be able to stay with the situation until something could be worked out. Instead, they might just walk away feeling angry and upset. Our goal in this type of situation is to help the individual keep his anxiety down and provide him with some verbal skills that will increase the probability of his request being satisfied.

Social approach or request responses with friends and intimate relationships

Compliments

Visualize yourself complimenting someone you know. The compliment can be on the way the person is dressed or some other nice thing you have observed him doing.

Now imagine that someone is complimenting you. How do you respond to this praise?

Were you able to give the compliment without feeling uneasy? Were you able to accept the compliment graciously without making excuses? Did you respond to "I really like your new outfit" with "Thank you" instead of "It is nothing really special" or "Someone else picked it out for me"? Giving and receiving compliments are two very important components of assertive behavior. Being able to give *genuine* "warm fuzzies" to another person without feeling uneasy allows you to become closer to that person. Likewise, it is important that you can accept compliments from others. Many individuals, from the time they are young children, are taught to be overly modest about their abilities

15

and achievements (possibly so that they do not risk offending others). One unfortunate result of this modesty when taken to extreme is that the individual is unable to accept complimentary statements from others and, in some cases, is not even able to acknowledge admirable qualities to himself. As a result of constantly refuting the compliments of others—"Your house really looks nice"/"That is only because the cleaning lady was here today"—the individual is less likely to get complimented in the future. People do not like to constantly have their compliments thrown back at them. When the compliments are no longer offered, the individual often begins to feel rejected or taken for granted. Assertion training does not attempt to turn the individual into a boastful braggart, but it does seek to help him accept and give compliments.

The neighbor—Part I
You are doing some work around your house and you realize that you are missing a tool to complete your job. You do not want to buy it at a store right now, and you remember that your neighbor has that tool. Visualize that you are now at your neighbor's house asking for the temporary loan of the tool.

The neighbor—Part II
Now assume that you are the neighbor who loaned the requested tool. However, several weeks have gone by, and it has still not been returned. In that you now need the tool yourself, you must go next door and ask for it to be returned. Visualize that scene.

Did you start off your conversation by saying, "I'm sorry, but. . .?" Did you get angry and make sarcastic comments to the person for not returning the article earlier? There is no need to be apologetic in this situation. Likewise, there is no reason to be abusive and violate the other person's self-respect in getting the item back.

This situation is one where the person is trying to satisfy a need. In some cases, the person might not ask for the item to begin with. Likewise, when seeking its return, he might respond by stuffing emotions and feeling angry rather than talking to the borrower. Both of these behaviors are nonassertive. Although you will not get each and every one of your needs met if you ask, you will get even less if you do not ask at all.

The nonverbal "warm fuzzy"

Imagine yourself sitting next to a friend towards whom you feel very positive. Without using any words, convey a warm positive feeling to this individual.

One of the most important aspects of assertion training is teaching the individual "social approach" behaviors. Many of these positive approach behaviors are conveyed by the words we use. However, there is also a wide variety of nonverbal behaviors that can be used to convey this message. Some of the more important nonverbal behaviors involve eye contact, body space, body posture, voice characteristics, and touching. Touching is an especially important behavior, and, yet, it is often avoided by close friends, couples, or parents. Recognizing that this is one of our biases, we feel that individuals who go through assertion training should feel more comfortable about their own bodies and their ability to reach out and make supportive or affectionate physical contact with others. With some cultural exceptions, positive physical contact is grossly underused in our society. We have a definite investment in trying to change this.

Protective or refusal responses
with strangers and situational relationships

Salesperson

Picture yourself answering your front door one evening and being confronted by a rather pushy salesperson who is trying to sell you a product. Although this is a product which you have purchased in the past (e.g., magazines, cookies, insurance), you do not have the interest or money to buy this product now. Assume that you cannot just shut the door—instead you must communicate to the person by what you say and how you say it that you are not interested.

Did you find yourself giving in when you did not really want to? Did you find yourself saying "I'm sorry" when, in fact, there is no need to apologize for something you do not want to do? If you ended up buying the merchandise which you did not really want, do you now resent the feeling that you were "forced" to do so?

Our purpose for not having you shut the door on the salesperson is to place you in a situation where you have to deal with a persistent individual. In an actual customer-salesperson interaction, it may be appropriate to shut the door when the salesperson chooses to ignore your message. However, in some cases, such as with a close friend who is asking you for something, there may be no physical door present to shut. When the other person does not listen to your refusal message, it may be very appropriate to employ some verbal protective skills, and to be able to do so without feeling extremely anxious or guilty.

Refusing donations

While you are at work one afternoon, a secretary from one of the other offices whom you do not know very well approaches you. The secretary tells you that one of your co-workers has just had a baby and that she, the secretary, is taking up a collection of $2 from each person in order to buy a nice gift for the new mother and baby. Your working inter-actions with the new mother have been very unpleasant over the past year. Reflecting on this for a moment, you feel that you do not wish to contribute to this collection fund even though you can well afford the $2. Your task is to politely refuse the request of the secretary who is standing before you and knows nothing about your previous interactions and feel-ings concerning the new mother.

Were you able to refuse the request without feeling guilty? Were you able to do so without degrading the new mother or telling the secretary a long detailed story about how you and the co-worker did not get along?

Protective or refusal responses
with friends and intimate relationships

Confidential information
You have been talking with someone who has given

you some confidential information about Gloria, a friend of yours with whom you work. Before this information was given, you agreed to keep the information confidential until the person could personally talk with Gloria and discuss the matter. It is now the next day and Gloria approaches you. She knows that you have discussed the situation with the other person, and she wants to know what was said. Your task is to try to keep this information confidential, as you have agreed to do. Gloria is making statements such as "If I am really your friend, you will tell me what was said," "I have told you information like this before under similar circumstances," and "You really are against me too." Visualize how you would handle this situation.

Did you give Gloria the information? Could you assertively say no to her and still keep Gloria's friendship? Was your anxiety extremely high? Did you feel extremely guilty for having hurt Gloria's feelings?

This is a situation where you are trying to refuse a friend a favor and still maintain a friendship. If you gave in, you may feel resentful because Gloria "manipulated you" into breaking a promise to someone else. On the other hand, if you did not give in, you may feel very guilty for not having come to Gloria's aid when she asked for your help. Gloria may be so upset that she thinks you do not like her and that you do not want to be her friend. You need to sort issues and clearly explain to Gloria that you would still like to be her friend, but that you feel committed to maintain the confidential information given to you.

We feel it is important for individuals to recognize that they have a right to refuse a request, especially if the request is not something the person wants to do or if the request is unwarranted. These assertive interactions with friends and intimates are typically more complex than with strangers because a stranger in a situational relationship is not as important to us as our friends. Consequently, we have more to lose if a friend's feelings are hurt by our assertive behaviors. Many nonassertive individuals worry that, if they hurt a friend's feelings by refusing a request, they will lose the friendship. We feel that part of being assertive in this kind of

situation is to work with the hurt feelings so that the friendship is, hopefully, not lost.

Criticism
Picture yourself being confronted by a friend/relative/
co-worker who seems to enjoy criticizing people—especially
you. You have concluded that this particular individual is not
really trying to help you, but, instead, engages in this activity
to obtain a one-up position. You have told this individual
before that you do not appreciate this behavior, and that you
would like it stopped. However, the person is now at it again.
Visualize the situation.

Did you know how to verbally stop the criticism? Was
your anxiety very high?

Here, again, is a situation where we feel an individual is
being victimized. Some individuals would continue taking the
criticism, say very little to the other person, and become very
upset inside. Other individuals might explode and verbally or
physically attack the other person. Both of these are inappropriate—especially since there are protective skills that an
individual can learn in order to protect himself and promote
a more equitable solution to the interaction. However, these
protective skills may cause a temporary or more permanent
break in the relationship; consequently, they should only be
used when the individual is aware of the risks in using these
protective skills and only *after* an open, honest, straight-
forward communication has failed.

Anger
You are busy at work when a friend/fellow employee/
boss comes in screaming at you in a very angry voice and calls
you names such as "stupid" and "incompetent." The person
is accusing you of making an error which proved to be very
costly and embarrassing to him. At this point, you're not even
certain if you made the error, but it is extremely difficult to
tell just what happened as long as the person is screaming and
carrying on in this manner. Visualize how you would handle
this situation, what you would do and say to the other
person, and where your anxiety is at.

Did you begin screaming back and calling the other person names? Did you remain silent but feel your anger skyrocket? Did you physically or verbally attack the other person? Did you notice your anxiety go up or down depending on how the situation developed?

Anger displayed by others is one of the more difficult emotional states to handle. Nevertheless, it is important that the recipient of the anger does not also lose his composure; otherwise the negative situation may become even worse. When this occurs, both people lose. There are certain behaviors that you can engage in which will tend to disarm the anger of the other person so that the situation can be discussed and the anger, hopefully, resolved. This, too, falls under the domain of assertion training.

These are all situations where assertive behaviors are appropriate. We would anticipate that an individual's anxiety would not be the same for each of these scenes; In fact, we would be very surprised if it were. In reality, some of the scenes described may be very easy for the person to carry out; whereas other situations may be very difficult or even out of the person's present behavioral repertoire.

Of interest to us as assertion trainers is the number of situations in which the individual experienced high levels of anxiety and/or was unable to find appropriate assertive actions and words to utilize. In Table 2 we have organized the fifteen vignettes of assertion into the 2x2 matrix we described in Table 1. As a final exercise, look at Table 2 on the following page and see if your own assertive difficulties can be localized into one or more of the four categories.

Table 2   *Assertive vignettes organized according to the interaction between assertive responses and levels of relationship*

	Social approach or request responses	Protective or refusal responses
Strangers and situational relationships	Eye contact Self-praise Introducing yourself Conversations In the restaurant The garage	Salesperson Refusing donations
Friends and intimate relationships	Compliments The neighbor (Parts I & II) The nonverbal "warm fuzzy"	Confidential information Criticism Anger

3 When assertion training is needed: Potential clients

Specific targets for assertion

In the previous chapter we described four types of inter-personal situations where assertive behaviors are appropriate. Within these four categories, the individual's response style can vary from being nonassertive to aggressive, with the assertive response style lying somewhere in between the two ends of this continuum. In addition, the person who is responding in a nonassertive or aggressive manner may be doing so because of unadaptively high levels of anxiety or because of a deficit in social skills. As an assertion trainer, it is important to understand and be able to differentiate each of these variables.

The nonassertive person

The nonassertive person, because of high levels of anxiety, guilt, or deficiencies in social skills, tends to bottle up emotions ranging from warmth to anger. As a result, this individual may experience difficulty in being able to do things such as ask for some need to be satisfied (e.g., "I want to make love tonight"); socialize comfortably with other people at work or at a party; speak up in a discussion and voice an opinion; express feelings or thoughts, positive or negative, to a friend, spouse, relative, or acquaintance; return some merchandise to a store; accept a compliment without refuting or demeaning the compliment; and so on. In addition, nonassertive individuals are often "victimized" by others in the sense that they cannot do things such as say "No" to an unreasonable request by someone else (e.g., Say "No" to a friend who wants to borrow a highly valued car;

23

say "No" to a pushy salesperson; refuse to watch a neighbor's kids when not really wanting to do this). They may also be unable to verbally protect themselves when someone is criticizing them or screaming at them unfairly. Nonassertive individuals tend to be overly apologetic, saying, "I'm sorry" a good deal of the time when they do not actually mean it. As a result, nonassertive individuals are often depressed, have a poor self-concept, and see themselves as being at the mercy of the world around them.

As a case in point, some neighbors of one of the authors recently had some uninvited house guests move in with them for "just a short time." This "short time" turned out to be three months, during which time the "guests" ate the neighbors' food without ever buying any of the groceries, drove the family car without filling up the empty gas tank, used the home phone for long distance calls denying they had made the calls, took over several rooms in the house to the point where one of the neighbors spent most of her time in the bedroom or at someone else's house, and then left without expressing much thanks, and indicated they would be back in a few weeks to pick up the rest of their clothes and belongings that were occupying two closets. Although these neighbors were extremely angry at what was happening, they never confronted the "guests" directly and weren't even certain if they could turn them down if they wanted to move in again at a later date!

The aggressive person

At the other end of the nonassertive/assertive/aggressive continuum, there are the aggressive individuals who do get more of their needs met, but often at the expense of someone else's dignity or self-respect. The aggressive person is someone who may explode at the slightest provocation and may be prone to physical fighting when angry or frustrated. The aggressive individual may also embarrass and put down others by name-calling or using obscenities when his needs are not being met. For example, at a restaurant the aggressive individual may scream at the waitress when the food is not served to his liking, whereas the nonassertive individual would be more likely to rationalize the situation, eat the food, and say nothing. The aggressive person dominates most conversations without letting others talk and continues to "attack" and criticize people even after they have tried to back away from the situation.

Aggressive individuals, like their nonassertive counterparts, may experience concern over their poor relationships with others. These people, too, may be experiencing high anxiety, guilt, or deficiencies in social skills. They may even be nonassertive in many situations, often hiding their feelings. However, when a number of these nonassertive experiences accumulate, they tend to lose control and explode at the next unsuspecting person who in any way angers or frustrates them. Whereas the nonassertive individual is frequently "victimized" by others and, consequently, may tend to avoid others, the aggressive individual is avoided by others who cannot predict or tolerate this behavior.

The end result is the same in the sense that both ends of the nonassertive/assertive/aggressive continuum leave the individual with few meaningful relationships. One of the basic goals then of assertion training is to help the individual find the middle ground between nonassertion and aggression where he can relate more effectively and successfully with other human beings, can be more responsive to others, and, at the same time, can acquire more personal needs and preserve feelings of self-worth.

An extremely important point to make is that assertion training is not the same as aggression training. Teaching an individual how to express his needs does not mean doing so at the expense of another person's self-respect and dignity. Unfortunately, many women, children, and adolescents who are acting assertively are seen by others or see themselves as being aggressive. It is equally unfortunate that some of these same individuals are not paid attention to when they are being appropriately assertive; consequently, they are provoked into responding aggressively in an attempt to get their needs met. Hopefully, as we learn to recognize our own basic rights and the rights of others, these situations will decrease in frequency.

Anxiety reduction

As previously stated, one of the basic goals of assertion training is to reduce anxiety which occurs in interpersonal situations. In fact, much of the original justification and impetus for using assertion training was derived from findings that assertive behaviors and interpersonal anxiety states were incompatible responses (Salter, 1949; Wolpe, 1958). Stop for a moment and try to think of some situation where you knew what you wanted to say or do; however, when you were confronted with the actual situation, you either became very anxious as you completed this transaction (rapid heart rate, sweaty palms, shaking, tightened stomach) or else you temporarily "froze" and forgot what to say or do. Most of us can recall instances where we became very anxious in carrying out some behavior, or where we thought of what to say or do only after the opportunity had passed. Whereas a certain amount of tension may be beneficial to alertness and performance, if the anxiety becomes too high, successful performance may actually be impeded. As such, we attempt to reduce unadaptive anxiety levels that may be interfering with assertive responses.

Whereas some clients are unaware that they are experiencing anxiety unless their anxiety becomes very high, others tend to confuse other emotions and feelings with their anxiety. For example, when a man is meeting an attractive woman, he may confuse arousal with distress. Likewise, when he is being unjustly criticized, he may confuse anger with anxiety. If anxiety is an interfering component of these emotions, then we would make an attempt to lower this anxiety. At the same time, however, we would not try to neutralize other feelings in these interactions. These other feelings may be quite normal and appropriate to the situation. Our aim is to assist the individual to reduce anxiety states that are inappropriate or interfering—not to shut off feelings altogether.

Skill training

There are also those individuals in assertion training who, even when their anxiety levels are low, do not know what to say or do in interpersonal situations. For these individuals, assertion training usually involves both skill training and anxiety reduction. It is rare to find an individual lacking in appropriate social skills to be free of interpersonal anxiety. Generally these socially inept people have attempted some social interactions in the past but have met with failure. These failure experiences are remembered and serve to sensitize the individual to the very skills in which he is deficient. It has been our experience that these individuals degrade themselves and see themselves as being stupid, awkward, or unworthy. The reality is that these individuals may be awkward because they are ignorant (i.e., lack skills) in the social situation. They confuse the fact that they make mistakes and are socially awkward with the reality that they can still be worthwhile and enjoyable people. A person with limited dating skills is not necessarily a bad or unlovable person. Rather, a person with limited dating skills is a person who does not know how to show how nice and lovable he can be. Consequently, we attempt to have our clients discriminate the difference between their worth and their skills.

As an example of skill training and anxiety reduction, we once spent the better part of one year training a group of high school and college-age individuals in a free clinic setting how to engage in more satisfying interpersonal relations with members of the opposite sex. Many of these individuals knew what to say or do when in the company of the opposite sex; however, their high anxiety levels prevented them from carrying out these actions effectively. Others in the same group did not even know how to go about making a date, how to start or maintain a conversation, or which behaviors the opposite sex generally considered to be complimentary or unsatisfactory. Generally, we have found that most individuals in assertion training require both anxiety reduction and skill training in helping them reach their desired goals. As such, both of these procedures can and should be taught simultaneously in assertion training.

Nonassertive myths

There are four myths we have identified in our assertion training groups. These myths are unwritten patterns of interacting with others that are common in this culture and which we believe are incompatible with our goals of teaching and promoting more open, honest, assertive relationships among people. We call these nonassertive response patterns "myths" because seldom, if ever, do individuals test the validity of the presupposed negative effects that the myths say will happen in a relationship. Secondly, these response styles have become so ingrained that, without our being fully aware of their influence, they are perpetuated and taught to others as being correct, important, and dangerous to act in ways not prescribed by the myths. Essentially, we feel that each of the four myths tends to place an individual in a one-down position where he will get fewer of his needs met in interpersonal relationships. In presenting these myths, our goals are to identify and define the nonassertive response styles or myths, describe specific reasons why we believe the myths promote feelings of dissatisfaction, and discuss assertion training procedures that can be utilized to dispel and counteract each of the myths presented here.

Myth of modesty

The first of our myths we have labeled the myth of modesty. This myth was touched upon previously in the "self-praise" and "compliment" assertion vignettes. An individual who subscribes to this myth finds it extremely difficult to praise himself or accept a compliment from someone else without refuting or demeaning the compliment. When taken to extreme, the individual is so tied into the belief system that "it is good to be modest at any cost" that he is not only unable to verbally accept compliments or give self-praise, but he also begins to deny the existence of any positive personal attributes. Such individuals are frequently found to be very self-critical, have a poor self-image, and they are often depressed.

An unfortunate result of this response style is that the individual tunes out or denies his positive attributes and begins to pay increasingly more attention to faults and criticism which just adds to the poor self-image and depression. These individuals often deny or feel uncomfortable when someone compliments them and then accept as "truth" any criticism that is directed their way. All of us have some faults and will be subject to criticism from others at one time or another. However, if we can also accept and feel that we have positive qualities which are worthy of praise, then it will be much easier to balance and put the criticisms in their proper perspective.

When working with compliment anxious individuals, our first goal is to help them recognize and acknowledge that they have some positive strengths and interests, even if these strengths and interests seem trivial or unrelated to assertive behavior (e.g., buying their own clothes, liking animals, enjoying science fiction stories). Secondly, we encourage them to share these strengths and interests with others while constantly emphasizing that through this sharing of positive strengths and interests, rather than weaknesses and failures, they are much more likely to establish more meaningful and enjoyable relationships. This is not to imply that we encourage these individuals to list all of their positive attributes to everyone they meet or to hold themselves up to another person so that the other person feels put down. However, selectively giving information about one's interests and strengths to others, especially when you do not know the other person very well, can serve to strengthen rather than weaken the relationship. An individual who can share some personal experiences, strengths, accomplishments, or joys, as well as elicit and actively listen to the personal experiences of others, is in a much better position than the individual who always sits quietly by and says nothing or only comments about the hardships and failures in his life. As a third stage, we teach the individual how to accept a compliment given to him without quickly discarding the compliment or making the other person feel that he had bad taste in giving the compliment in the first place.

Compliments and praise, whether given to oneself or by someone else, are some of the treasures in life which can make our existence and our relationships more enjoyable and meaningful. These "treasures" are needlessly lost when one discards them in order to maintain a cloak of modesty.

Myth of the good friend

A second common myth that we believe greatly interferes with closer interpersonal relationships and more satisfying communications is the myth of the good friend. This myth *assumes* that anyone who is a good friend, or spouse, or relative, or neighbor, or boss, or salesperson, should be able to anticipate our needs, our feelings, our thoughts, and give us what we would like to have—without our clearly saying what those needs are. How many times have you heard yourself or someone else say, "If he really was a friend, he would have known that I do not like. . ." or "If she really loved me, she would. . ."? We often expect others to be able to accurately read our thoughts and feelings and then respond accordingly. Unfortunately, most people are not very good at this, including most therapists. In that you are the only person who really knows what is going on inside your head or your guts at any given moment in time, it becomes *your* responsibility to let others know what you are feeling and thinking. For if you do not verbally and specifically communicate what you want, expect, resent, appreciate, or feel hurt by, the other person may never respond in a manner that satisfies you. As a result, resentment may begin to grow on your part until you either "blow up" at the individual or begin to avoid him more and more.

For example, a friend may constantly ask you to watch her children for the afternoon or to drive her across town because she does not like to drive on the freeways. You may feel this is an imposition on your time, and you may, in fact, give some indirect communication of this feeling through your response (e.g., "Well, I guess that will be all right if there is no one else for you to ask," or "I was planning on going out to lunch that day with my cousin, but I guess I could help you out"). However, if you do not clearly state your objections or your other plans, the individual may conclude that it is not an imposition of your time at all; consequently, requests such as this may occur over and over again. Likewise, if you want to take a Saturday morning off to go shopping while your spouse watches the kids, it is your responsibility to tell your spouse this and not to expect that he will see that you are tired of watching the kids and need some time for yourself.

Those who subscribe to the myth of the good friend usually behave according to its dictates in many levels of their relationships. They typically do not state clearly what they want, and consequently, they feel they are being abused or taken advantage of by others. If you were ever at a restaurant where the food was served cold and found yourself angry and complaining under your breath, you may have been subscribing to the myth of the good friend. The assumption here is that if it were a "good" waiter or waitress, the person would know that the food was served improperly. If you have ever secretly wished that your spouse or lover remember your birthday, you may be buying into the good friend myth. In this case, a "good" spouse or lover would know how important this date is to you and would respond accordingly. However, it is our belief that in such cases it is *your* responsibility to make it clear to the other person just what you are feeling and what you would like the individual to do in this situation.

Part of the myth, and a common erroneous assumption, is that the values you hold to be important must be held in equal importance by others. This is not always the case. For example, one of the authors has typically been unconcerned about being places on time unless it is *clearly* understood that prompt attendance is important to that situation. However, the other author typically arrives on time to most situations as a matter of habit and assumes that when a business or social date is made, he and the others will consider the time commitment as an important aspect of the date. Only after some open communications were given did we realize that each of us had a different value and definition of promptness. Equally as important, neither of us was "wrong" in terms of our actions based upon our individual belief systems and values.

We believe that individuals who frequently employ a response style consistent with that of the myth of the good friend are, at least in one sense, nonassertive. As a result of this nonassertive behavior, the individual often attempts to rationalize and project the responsibility of communication to other people in his life. Often these individuals complain that they are just not able to find people who understand them. They spend a good part of their lives with unfulfilled wants and needs searching for "the perfect person." This fantasized "perfect person" turns out to be someone who is able to anticipate and provide for their needs without words or communications. We feel that there is no such "perfect person" and that the open and honest communications of our needs is crucial in all relationships. It is true that as a relationship continues to develop, the other person will be able to accurately anticipate or predict your feelings and wants on some occasions. However, in most cases, this only occurs after you have expressed personal feelings and wants on several occasions in the past.

At times members in our groups have stated that it would do no good to be assertive, because nothing they could do or say would make the other person change. That is actually a true statement. There may not be anything a person can do or say that will make the other person change. However, if changes were never possible, then there would be no real purpose for doing psychotherapy, counseling, or training in the first place. Our contention is that one of the ways people change is through clear feedback, and that individuals in healthy relationships will change for each other when there is understanding and respect for each other's needs.

Unfortunately, there are those individuals in search of the "perfect person," who find it difficult to accept change from the other person even when it does occur. When there is a change following an assertive response, these individuals find it unacceptable because the other person did not give them what they wanted without being told and, by being told, it now loses its value. Have you ever heard someone else remark, "If I tell him my birthday is important to me and he is nice to me on that day, it is only because I asked him and not because he really cared for me"? These individuals are placing themselves in a position where they cannot possibly win. Often they fail to ask for their needs to be satisfied, thereby feeling hurt and angry. If they do ask and their requests are met, they still are not satisfied. We believe that only when one lets others know what his wants and feelings are and accepts the possibility that it is not the "duty" of the other person to know and respond accordingly without this feedback, will the individual be able to avoid the detrimental results of the myth of the good friend.

Myth of anxiety

The third nonassertive myth is the myth of anxiety. Essentially, people who attempt to live their lives within this myth are phobic of their own anxiety and phobic of revealing that they are anxious in interpersonal situations. They fear others noticing their anxiety because they believe that to be anxious shows others that there is something terribly wrong with them or that they are "weak" individuals. The stereotype of the "Great American Male" who is unafraid and unaffected by anything in his environment is the tragic "hero" of the myth of anxiety. Men who subscribe to this myth often feel prevented from expressing their emotions when they are anxious. An example of such a person is a client who had an intense fear of flying. Unfortunately, he was unable to avoid flying since his job required him to travel over long distances within very short periods of time. Consistent with the myth, he saw himself as being unable to express his fear, ask for some help, or ask for a transfer to another position. He felt that to do any of these would place him in the position of being seen as a coward or sissy by his fellow employees. He finally sought professional help after tolerating his high anxiety for over fifteen years. During these fifteen years, he had not shared this fear with anyone but his wife. He was afraid to tell his grown children, relatives, friends, employer, or fellow employees that he was anxious. He was the tragic "hero" in the myth of anxiety since he was unable for years to assert himself enough to ask others for help with his problem.

One of the detrimental effects of this myth is that individuals who are suffering from its influence often spend a great deal of energy trying to conceal their anxiety from others. However, in many cases, this concern to "look good" actually increases the anxiety level. For example, giving a talk before a large group of people or before a group of critical peers can be a very anxiety producing task for many individuals. As the individual begins to speak, he may be aware of anxiety symptoms such as a cracking voice, sweaty palms, or trembling hands. At this point he can engage in some activity to counteract the anxiety such as relaxation. He can also acknowledge his tension to the audience, thereby reducing much of the energy and tension expended in trying to look calm and collected. If the former relaxation procedure does not work and the latter self-disclosure procedure is used, the person often reports an immediate release of tension and anxiety. However, if the person tries to hide this anxiety by powering through it, he often becomes increasingly more sensitive to each additional anxiety cue, and, as a result, becomes increasingly more anxious in the situation.

Everyone experiences anxiety at times, and anxiety can be a normal emotional response in some situations. At other times, however, this anxiety response may be irrational, unadaptive or inappropriate to the situation at hand, and, in such instances, the individual may wish to seek some help for this phobia. However, even if the anxiety response is irrational, unadaptive or inappropriate, we find no good reason for being ashamed of its existence or trying to keep it locked up inside of us for fear of being seen as weak or inadequate.

In the course of assertion training, those individuals with the myth of anxiety are encouraged to begin sharing their feelings of tension when they begin to occur. By sharing these feelings in a frequent and ongoing manner, we desensitize the individual to the fear of having and trying to hide anxiety. When this is accomplished, the person can then begin to deal with the feared stimulus itself in a more appropriate and effective manner.

Myth of obligation

The fourth myth that we would like to identify and dispel is the myth of obligation. This myth can be divided into two parts. The first part assumes that if a person asks a friend for a favor, in order for the friendship to con-

34

tinue, the friend is obligated to grant the request. Essentially, there appears to be little or no possibility for a refusal in a friendship according to this myth. Individuals who never seem to say "No" are often seen as happy-go-lucky people who are always smiling and are always ready to help a friend. Others may frequently call on them for favors since they never refuse and never express that they are feeling imposed upon. Our experience has been that these individuals often do feel imposed upon, and they feel quite resentful that others keep asking them for favors. However, they do not assert themselves and refuse any requests, for they fear that they will hurt their friends' feelings and, consequently, their friends will not like them anymore.

The second part of the myth of obligation equates making a request of someone with an imposition. The individual feels that the other person would not be able to refuse the request, so rather than imposing on the person and possibly making him angry and resentful, the request is not made in the first place. As a result, the individual who avoids making requests may have many unfulfilled needs.

A relationship between two people acting consistently within the myth of obligation is one in which:

Jack doesn't say no to Jill
because she will resent him,
so he resents her.

Jill doesn't say no to Jack
because he will resent her,
so she resents him.

Jack doesn't ask Jill
because she will resent him,
so he resents her.

Jill doesn't ask Jack
because he will resent her,
so she resents him.

Jack and Jill aren't talking anymore.
They resent each other too much.

We have seen several individuals who subscribe to the myth of obligation and, consequently, feel resentful and unfulfilled in their relationships. In assertion training, our goal is to dispel this myth by teaching people how to comfortably request and refuse things in a relationship without feeling guilty. The reality is that when both parties know that each is capable of making a request or a refusal, they tend to trust the other person's decisions more, and the relationship becomes even closer.

Benefiting a wide range of clients

We believe that almost everyone can gain some benefit from either the philosophy or the procedures of assertion training. Since we live in a world where most of us must depend upon others for even our basic necessities in life (such as food, living quarters, medical care), it seems almost self-evident that any procedures that will enhance one's ability to interact more successfully with others will be of some value. Assertion training has been used with hospitalized patients, out-patients, couples, women's groups, children, adolescents, school administrators, factory workers, business people, and college students. The content and focus of what is taught may differ from group to group; however, the overall goal of enhancing a person's self-worth and his ability to better survive in a socialized society is a common theme running throughout most of the published works in this area.

Over the past few years we have observed a surging interest in assertion training for adolescents, single young adults, and especially women. Perhaps it is very rightly so that these three populations are taking a close look at assertion training, for it is through procedures such as these that they will, hopefully, be able to obtain more self-awareness, freedom, recognition, and equality in our society.

It is our belief that each and every one of us can benefit from being assertive. Likewise, those individuals who work with others, especially in a supervisory or training capacity (e.g., therapists, teachers, parents, training managers) are in an excellent position to teach others assertive behaviors—both by what they model themselves and by some of the systematic procedures described in this book.

Part 2 The fundamentals
of <u>assertion training</u>

4 The assessment interview and the initial focus of treatment

How do you select individuals who would benefit from assertion training as opposed to some other form of treatment? Sometimes a client will specifically ask for assertion training. More often, you must yourself determine the need for some assertion training with those clients who come in to see you for a variety of reasons. One aspect of this assessment and screening process involves an in-depth interview, including a behavioral repertoire assessment. In conducting the interview, keep in mind that no one acts assertively all of the time; consequently, determining the need for some assertive training becomes a matter of *how often* and *under what circumstances* the individual responds in a nonassertive and/or aggressive manner.

The assessment interview

In conducting the initial interview, and in other stages of therapy as well, it is important to pay close attention to the actual content of what is being said as well as the manner in which this information is being given. The information being conveyed through the content may coincide with what you observe during the interview; however, in other cases, there may be a disparity between what a person is saying occurs and what he is doing (e.g., the individual may describe himself as having no trouble talking to people for the first time, yet he may be visibly trembling and giving you poor eye contact while telling you this). Both what you hear and what you see are important sources of information which need to be discussed and evaluated with the client.

With respect to the content, we ask a number of behaviorally oriented questions which can have a direct bearing on the individual's nonassertive/assertive/aggressive behaviors. Some of the more basic questions involve what the client sees as his presenting problem(s); the extent to which this problem exists (e.g., how often the problem occurs, under what circumstances it occurs, its duration and magnitude, the consequences); and the goals which the individual is seeking to achieve as a result of seeking help at this time. When a specific problem can be identified, an attempt is made to determine and better understand the historical etiology for the problem; however, proportionally more time is spent trying to identify the current situational determinants for the behavior than how the problem got started in the first place.

The following is a composite interview between a therapist (Th) and a nonassertive client (Cl).

Th: I would like to begin by asking you to tell me what you see as the major problem area for which you are seeking some assistance.

Cl: I have been feeling very nervous lately, and I thought if I did not see someone soon, I would become a basket case.

Th: It sounds as if your nervousness is really troubling you. Can you be more specific as to what you mean by nervous?

Cl: Well, for one thing, I find that my hands shake so much at work lately that I often have to stop what I am doing and leave my desk for awhile.

Th: In addition to feeling shaky at work, are you aware of any other things that happen to you when you are nervous?

Cl: I forget what I want to say at times and often I will break out in a cold sweat. Things have gotten so bad lately that I don't even feel like going to work in the morning.

Th: I suspect that must be a disturbing feeling—especially if work was something that you used to look forward to and enjoy. When you are feeling very nervous, do you ever notice that your heart is pounding faster or that you feel light-headed?

Cl: Yes, both of those things happen, too.

Th: Some of what you are describing sounds like an anxiety type of reaction, and these reactions can be both frightening and frustrating. I would like to know just how nervous you are feeling right at this very moment. If you were to rank yourself on a scale from 0 to 100, with 0 representing a state of complete relaxation such as you might feel just prior to falling asleep or after taking a nice warm bath and 100 representing a state of panic, where would you place yourself on that continuum right at this moment?

Cl: About 40.

Note: This is an excellent place to evaluate if what the client says corresponds to what the therapist sees. It also can be helpful in evaluating how uncomfortable the client is feeling about the interview itself.

Th: Where would you put yourself on that scale when you are at work?

Cl: Well, the other day when my boss asked me to stay after work and finish up a report that wasn't due for at least another week, I would have ranked myself at 95.

Th: That sounds pretty high. Do you have any idea why your anxiety was so high in that situation?

Cl: Well, to begin with, I had a ticket to go to the theater with some friends that night. Besides, I did not think it was fair of him to ask me to do such a rush job on a report that was not originally due until next week.

Th: It sounds like you felt your boss was taking advantage of you. Did you say anything to your boss when this incident occurred?

Cl: No, I just stayed after work and called my friends to tell them I could not make it that night.

Th: So you gave up a night of enjoyment and being with friends in order to work. Looking back on that situation, how do you feel about what happened?

Cl: I am really feeling angry. First of all, I am angry at myself for not being able to stand up to my boss. Secondly, I am angry at my boss for even asking me. What is even worse, he didn't even thank me for staying late!

Th: So even after you helped out, you received no verbal appreciation from your boss. Do situations like this with your boss happen very often?

Cl: Yes, I'm afraid so. I really do not know how to deal with him without getting upset or just giving in.

Th: Are there other people at work with whom you are having difficulty in addition to your boss?

Cl: Well, I guess I am pretty much of a loner at work. I don't talk much with the other employees because I feel awkward and self-conscious. However, my boss is the main person I feel nervous around.

Note: This is probably because the client can avoid the other people at work more easily.

Th: It sounds as if you are pretty isolated at your job. How long has this situation been going on, you being a loner at work and having trouble with your boss?

Cl: I have been a loner for a long time, probably most of my life. However, the situation has gotten much worse since I moved to this new company eight months ago.

Th: Moving can often be very difficult for an individual to deal with. At least, I know that moving and the separation from familiar people and places is difficult for me. You have mentioned one incident at work that made you very nervous. About how many times during the course of a week would you estimate your anxiety level goes over 50 on that scale we just talked about?

Cl: I'd say at least three or four times a week, maybe even more.

Note: This would be one of the areas where some baseline data would be helpful.

Th: The way you say that and emphasize the "at least," it sounds like three to four times a week is a conservative estimate. Is there anyone at work you feel comfortable with or can tell how you are feeling?

Cl: There is one other employee who works in another office nearby with whom I have become friendly and can share some of my feelings, but she's the only one. Outside of work there are a couple of people whom I can talk with, but by the time I get home in the evening my stomach is already in knots.

Th: It's nice that you have found at least one other person at work with whom you can talk in order to relieve some of that initial pressure. It is also nice that you have some individuals outside of work with whom you feel comfortable enough to share some personal experiences and feelings with. Of course, I think in the long run it is much more effective if you can learn to deal directly with the person who is contributing to your feeling upset. At the present time I am hearing that you do not deal directly with the person who somehow upsets you—at least not at work. Just how do you deal with the situation other than becoming anxious and occasionally leaving your desk?

Cl: Lately, I have been taking tranquilizers two or three times a day, but when that doesn't do the job, I just make up some excuse that I am sick and go home for the day. However, I don't think I want to do that much longer.

Th: I agree with you that taking tranquilizers daily or leaving work does not sound like a very good long-range solution. At this time, are you able to identify some short-range or long-range goals as to how you would like to respond differently in this new job of yours?

43

CL: To begin with, I would like to stand up to my boss more so that he does not keep taking advantage of me. I work hard and put in a good day's work, so there is no reason I should feel so anxious when he is around or be unable to tell him that I have other plans when he asks me to work late on such short notice.

Note: The client has given information here which may indicate that some desensitization to the boss' presence is needed as well as teaching some assertive behaviors which will enable the client to deal more openly and honestly with the boss.

Th: If I understand you correctly, you are saying that you would like to be able to relate better to your boss without feeling anxious and without feeling that you are being taken advantage of. That sounds like a very reasonable goal. Are there any other job-related goals that you have at the present time?

CL: I'd also like to know more of my fellow employees and feel more comfortable around them. I guess I never was very good at getting to meet new people. I just don't know what to say or how to carry on a good conversation.

Th: It sounds as if you have been able to meet at least one person at work with whom you have been able to establish some verbal interaction, and you did mention that there were some outside friends you were planning on going to the theater with before your boss came on the scene. That's a good start. With respect to your boss and getting to know some other people at work, I think it will be possible to help you reduce much of your anxiety without tranquilizers and without having to go home from work. In addition, it sounds as if you would benefit from some assertive skills which are designed to help individuals be more open with their feelings—that includes more open and honest with your boss as well as learning some conversation skills to help you in meeting new people.

Cl: Sounds good.

Th: We have talked thus far pretty much about your work situation. Do you find yourself becoming nervous in other situations as well, such as at home?

Cl: I don't think there are any major problems with my family that wouldn't be cleared up if my job situation improved. However, I am having some problems with my fifteen-year-old daughter lately.

Th: Young adults can be a real challenge at times. Please try to tell me a little more about this.

Cl: Well, just last week my daughter asked if she could stay out past twelve midnight on Friday night. I told her that she was still too young to stay out that late, but she proceeded to argue with me.

Th: From having children of my own, I know that situation well. What happened?

Cl: I said "No" twice, and that should have been final. I will not tolerate a fifteen-year-old who talks back to her parents, telling them what all of her friends are doing. When she kept insisting that she should be allowed to stay out late and then proceeded to call me "a selfish old prude" I grounded her for the month and took away her telephone privileges.

Note: In this case there is an indication that both the parent and the daughter might benefit from some assertion training whereby both parties would be better able to express their feelings and possibly work out a more mutually satisfying arrangement without infringing upon the dignity of the other person through name-calling or the excessive use of parental power.

Th: It sounds as if you both got pretty upset over that matter. How do you feel about the whole thing now?

Cl: Under the circumstances, I think we both lost. I did not like screaming, being called names, and getting upset—

after all, I can do that at work. As for my daughter, I know she is not happy with having to stay at home for a month without being able to use the telephone. I guess I would like to be able to communicate better with my daughter—if that is at all possible.

The interview would continue along similar lines, with the therapist attempting to elicit as much information as possible on the parameters of the presenting problem(s). At some points, if the client described a situation where needs were not being met or assertive responses were not being made, the therapist might have the individual do some role-playing (e.g., the interaction with the boss or daughter in the previous interview). The therapist would first play the role of the "significant other" to see how the client responds to this situation. Then the therapist would switch roles and play the part of the client—modeling a more assertive response style—while the client played the role of the significant other. This would be followed by the client taking his own role again, only this time, hopefully, in a more assertive manner. This enables the client to obtain a better understanding of what assertion training involves. For example, returning to the client's description of the interaction with the boss, the therapist might have the client describe just what was said in the interaction and then role-play the situation. The therapist might then give the client an alternative response style to consider.

Th: Now, for a moment, Pat, I would like you to assume that you are the boss asking me to stay late tonight and work. Given what you have already told me before about wanting to go to the theater, I will play the role of you and model one way you might want to consider responding to your boss if such a situation were to occur again in the future. Before we begin, do you have any questions?

Cl: No.

Th: How anxious are you feeling right at this moment on that zero to one hundred point scale?

46

Cl: About 20.

Th: OK. Since your anxiety is not very high, I want you to assume the role of your boss and let's see what happens.

Cl: (Playing the role as the boss) Pat, we need this report out sooner than I had originally anticipated. I'd like you to stay here tonight and do some work on this.

Th: (Playing the role of the client named Pat) Boss, I can certainly try to rearrange my schedule in order to work on this report earlier than I had expected; however, tonight I have already made some other plans which I'd really like to keep.

Cl: Well, Pat, it's very important that this job get done now.

Th: I can understand your need to have this report done early and I'm certainly not trying to avoid doing the work if you want me to change my work schedule. However, at the same time, I'd like to do what I had planned for this evening. When do you need the report?

Cl: By the end of the week at the latest.

Th: I don't see any reason why that deadline cannot be met if I reshuffle my time around a bit. How about if I work on the report all day tomorrow? If I'm not satisfied with where I am at by 5:00 tomorrow, I will make plans to stay after work tomorrow and try to finish it up. That way I'll be able to go ahead with my plans for tonight and you'll have your report by Friday.

Cl: Well, if you think you can get it done in time, I guess that would be all right. But I want you to understand that it must be done by Friday.

Th: I'll do everything I can to see that it's completed on time—even if it means staying after work tomorrow.

Cl: Well, OK. Have a nice time tonight and let me know how you are coming along on the report tomorrow afternoon.

Th: OK, I'll do that, and thank you for not insisting that I give up my plans for this evening.

Note: Pat never did tell the boss what the plans were—they were important to Pat and that is all that matters. Also, the issue was not brought up here about the boss giving Pat a rush order without advance notice or about the lack of appreciation for Pat's willingness to work late one evening. These issues might best be brought up sometime in the near future when neither Pat nor the boss is feeling so rushed.

As illustrated in the interview with the client, the therapist begins at a very early stage to focus attention on specific issues and begins setting some initial behavioral goals for dealing with these issues more successfully.

When a client describes a situation in which he is not getting his needs met, some attention is given to the value he places on his own feelings, needs, and actions; what other individuals figure in his life; and how he interacts with these "significant others" in terms of satisfying personal needs and wants. An assessment is made of the individual's success in meeting these needs across a wide variety of situations—from starting a conversation with someone the individual would like to know better, to saying "No" to a close friend. By carefully listening to how the client describes himself and his interactions with others (or lack of them), you can usually detect clear evidence of anxiety, deficit behaviors, nonassertive behaviors, or aggressive behaviors which may be occurring on either a situational or generalized basis.

In addition to what the person says, the manner in which the information is conveyed is also important. The interview itself can be used to identify verbal and nonverbal characteristics frequently found in nonassertive, assertive, and aggressive individuals. For example, poor eye contact, timid voice, body posture, and anxiety responses such as shaking or sweating are all important guideposts in conducting the initial interview. Another assessment alternative (which we have not personally used) involves presenting the client with several audio- or video-taped situations, and then observing and discussing how the client would respond to these "canned" situations (McFall & Marston, 1970; McFall

& Lillesand, 1971; McFall & Twentyman, 1973; Eisler, Miller & Hersen, 1973).

The initial focus of treatment

If nonassertive or aggressive behaviors constitute an important part of the client's presenting problem and if we feel some assertion training may be appropriate, the next question is where does one begin treatment. Do you immediately begin teaching the client how to deal more satisfactorily with those individuals or events in the client's life that are causing him the greatest amount of difficulty and for which he has sought your help, or do you approach the handling of these high stress provoking events through the practice of other situations that are, perhaps, several steps removed from the main problems?

Unfortunately, there is no simple answer to this question. Where you begin treatment depends largely upon the particular circumstances and needs of the individual, upon the severity and extent of the problem, and the degree of anxiety present. There is, however, a general rule which may be of considerable help in determining where you begin: *Start with something simple where the probability of success is very high and the anxiety is very low.* Our experience has been that most clients want to immediately start work on their most difficult problem. Although this tendency is certainly understandable from the client's perspective, the danger exists that initial assertive attempts may meet with failure until the client is able to sufficiently reduce anxiety and master certain interpersonal skills. If this failure experience occurs with major issues or with significant people in the client's environment, then the client may needlessly jeopardize a close relationship and may be more anxious and reluctant to assertively face the situation again in the future. Consequently, although we may do some initial role-playing of the more difficult situations in order to show the direction in which we will be moving, our tendency is to postpone the bigger problems for awhile and work with the less volatile situations until the client has experienced some degree of efficiency and success with his newly acquired assertive

49

behaviors. In some ways, it is like starting to repaint a house for the first time. Rather than start the person with the largest and most difficult room to paint, we start him with a smaller room where his painting skills can be mastered and where his mistakes are less important and less conspicuous.

Initially, we try to get to know the person as well as possible. By this we mean that we try to identify the minor as well as the major issues that are bothering him. This involves determining whether the individual is generally non-assertive/aggressive or whether he is having problems with specific situations. It also involves determining if his assertive difficulties lie more with approach/request situations than with protective/refusal situations, and whether it is more difficult to be assertive with intimate relationships than it is with casual situational relationships. Furthermore, we are interested in determining just how much of the individual's assertion difficulties are caused by a lack of appropriate social skills as opposed to high anxiety. We do not begin treatment by asking the individual to change any of his non-assertive/aggressive behaviors. On the contrary, we ask the person to avoid trying anything new until the assessment phase is completed and until some baseline data has been collected.

The assessment phase not only involves the person-to-person interviews, but also a number of self-report, paper-and-pencil measures which constitute our Assertive Data Collection Package discussed in the following chapter.

5 Preliminary activities

The Assertive Data Collection Package (ADCP)

The Assertive Data Collection Package (ADCP) consists of several self-report, paper-and-pencil measures which we utilize in the initial assessment phase of treatment in order to determine the extent of the individual's assertive difficulties and, again, throughout the treatment period in order to monitor the progress that is being made. Some of the forms and questionnaires we use come from the work of others, whereas other measures we are presenting here (i.e., SUDS Diary, Assertion Training Diary, Assertive Goal Scale, Homework Diary) have been developed from our own training experiences. All of these measures require the client to monitor and report on various situations that are occurring in his life and which are related to assertive situations or high anxiety states.

One of our goals in utilizing the ADCP is to increase the accuracy of the data collected in the client's environment. Before we began asking our clients to keep written records, we found that the information they gave about things that had occurred during the previous week was sometimes sketchy and distorted. For example, an individual who was depressed on the day of the training session due to a fight with his spouse reported little assertive success during the previous week. Because of the intensity and recency of the fight, the individual did not mention that a raise was requested at work, a high pressure salesperson was successfully handled, and an enjoyable conversation with the person's spouse took place earlier in the week. By asking the individual to keep daily records, a much clearer and complete picture of what has transpired during the past week both in terms of failures as well as success experiences is obtained.

The ADCP deals primarily with assertion-related issues that are currently taking place in the individual's life space. However, it also takes into consideration past performance and future goals. For example, the assertive questionnaires, which are used during the initial assessment phase of training, deal largely with past events, whereas the Assertion Training Diary, the Assertive Goal Scale, and the Homework Diary each contain sections dealing with future goals of the client.

The ADCP is designed within a behavioral framework. These self-report measures call for clear, explicit descriptions of behaviors which are both observable and measurable. For example, anxiety levels are presented in a numerical, quantifiable manner on the Assertion Training Diary and on the Homework Diary. Also, the homework assignments and the assertive goals (on the Assertion Training Diary, the Assertive Goal Scale, and the Homework Diary) can be statistically evaluated as having been met successfully or unsuccessfully.

In addition to providing meaningful data, the ADCP also helps to reduce some of the magical qualities sometimes associated with psychotherapy. By becoming an active and contributing participant in the data collection process, the client need not see himself as being a helpless and dependent person who must totally rely on the trainer's responses in order to give direction and evaluate improvement. Also, by becoming more aware of the many variables covered in the ADCP, it is our belief that the individual will be better able to function on his own once the formal assertion training procedure has ended.

The trainer who wishes to use the ADCP faces two immediate tasks. The first task is to teach the client how to monitor his behaviors and fill out the different ADCP measures. Unless the first step is completed successfully, there will be little opportunity for later interpretation and utilization of client information.

In utilizing the ADCP, it becomes the primary responsibility of the client to monitor and record in an accurate and precise manner those situations which are related to the assertion training program. This is not an easy task in that the client is being asked to write explicit behavioral descriptions of situations in which he may be quite emotionally involved. Yet, these descriptions are to be clear and accurate. Based upon the information supplied on these forms, it should be possible to set up and role-play selected situations during the group meetings. For those readers who have had little prior experience with having clients monitor and describe their own behaviors outside of the therapy session, the writings of Goldfried & Merbaum (1973) and Mager (1962) are strongly recommended. Also, in asking clients to monitor and describe their own behaviors outside of group, it is recommended that this recording be done as soon as possible after the situation has occurred in order to reduce distortions caused by the passage of time.

The second task of the trainer using the ADCP is the interpretation and utilization of the information supplied by the client on the various forms. The ADCP has been divided into five segments with each segment corresponding to a different period of the assertion training process. The five segments of the ADCP include defining assertion and obtaining information on assertive response styles, learning about anxiety and how to measure it, obtaining baseline data and building hierarchies with respect to present assertive skills, setting treatment goals, and practicing and monitoring new assertive skills. In Table 3 we have listed each of these segments together with the corresponding measures from the ADCP which we utilize. (Appendix B presents blank ADCP recording forms.)

In the following pages, we will describe each of these segments together with the hand-outs that are given to the client during these time periods. It should be noted that trainers working with certain populations (e.g., young children, mentally retarded, severely emotionally disturbed) may not be able to utilize these ADCP measures in the manner we have described. The trainer may need to assume the responsibility of monitoring and recording specific behaviors based upon direct interaction with the client, or this task may need to be given to someone else in the client's immediate environment.

53

Table 3 *Assertion training segments and corresponding ADCP measures*

Assertion training segments	ADCP measures utilized
1. Obtaining information on assertive response styles	Assertion Questionnaires
2. Learning about anxiety and how to measure it	The Subjective Units of Discomfort Scale SUDS Diary
3. Obtaining baseline data and building hierarchies with respect to present assertion skills	Assertion Training Diary (ATD)
4. Setting treatment goals	Assertive Goal Scale (AGS)
5. Practicing and monitoring new assertive skills	Homework Diary

Obtaining information on assertive response styles

Much of the initial discussion, definition, and description of the parameters of appropriate assertive behaviors is carried out during the intake interviews with the client. It is at this time that we begin assessing the appropriateness of some assertive training and discuss this possibility with the client. We attempt to give the client an experiential understanding of what assertion training is about through some role-playing experiences during the first interviews. In terms of a brief, written description of what assertion training encompasses, we are finding that the one-page description of assertion training by Grimes, Moser & Smith (1975) is extremely useful (see Appendix A). For those who find reading to be an enjoyable activity rather than a laborious task, we frequently recommend one or more books that are directly related to some of the material we cover during the assertion training process. At the present time, these books include *Your Perfect Right* (Alberti & Emmons, 1974);

The Assertive Woman (Phelps & Austin, 1975); *Stand Up, Speak Out, Talk Back* (Alberti & Emmons, 1975); *Don't Say Yes When You Want To Say No* (Fensterheim & Baer, 1975); *How To Be Your Own Best Friend* (Newman & Berkowitz, 1971); and *Conditioned Reflex Therapy* (Salter, 1949).

Assertion questionnaires

To further help the client understand the parameters of assertive behavior and to acquire some additional information we might have missed during the initial interview, we give the client one or more assertive questionnaires. There are actually a number of paper-and-pencil self-report measures which may be useful for these purposes. Prior to the development of specific assertive questionnaires, the *Willoughby Neuroticism Schedule* (1934) and the Wolpe-Lang *Fear Survey Schedule* (1964) were often used to identify individuals in need of assertion training (Wolpe, 1958, 1969; Wolpe & Lazarus, 1966; Cotler, 1975). More recently, however, a number of scales and questionnaires specifically designed to identify nonassertive/aggressive behaviors have been developed. These scales include the Wolpe-Lazarus *Assertion Questionnaire* (1966), the *Lawrence Assertive Inventory* (1970), the *Constriction Scale* (Bates & Zimmerman, 1971), the *Conflict Resolution Inventory* (Gambrill & Richey, 1972), the *Rathus Assertiveness Schedule* (1973a), the *Behavioral Assertiveness Test* (Eisler, Miller & Hersen, 1973) and the Alberti & Emmons *Assertive Inventory* (1974).

As a representative example of an assertion questionnaire which can be used with an adult population, we have included a copy of the questionnaire we are presently using as part of our ADCP (Appendix B). As can be readily seen by those who are familiar with other assertive paper-and-pencil questionnaires, our form is very similar (or identical) with respect to many of the questions asked and the areas of information tapped.

Although there are a number of these scales now available and probably more on the way, there are certain cautions and limitations in using each of them. To begin with, much of the content in these scales stresses nonassertive and/or high anxiety situations rather than situations where the individual is aggressive or lacking in some specific skill. (The Alberti & Emmons, 1974 and Gambrill & Richey, 1972 scales are somewhat better in this respect.) Secondly, many of the scales have been designed to fit the problems of specific populations (e.g., college students, private patients); consequently, one must be cautious of overgeneralization.

However, our major concern rests with how the scale scores are often interpreted and used. It is our opinion that, at this time, it is a mistake to look at scores alone without going over each individual item with the client. Although this takes considerably more time and may not be feasible when screening large numbers of individuals for research purposes, we have repeatedly found that clients tend to misinterpret several of the questions. Only after going over and discussing the individual items with the client do we feel comfortable in making more definitive statements as to what the results seem to indicate. Another somewhat related issue involves the interpretation of any given scale score. It is probably true that individuals who obtain a very high nonassertive/aggressive score are in need of some kind of assistance—assuming that the items were interpreted correctly in the first place; however, what about the individual who receives a low score but is nonassertive/aggressive on some "critical" items? Although many of the questions on these scales tend to cluster, as indicated by factor analysis, we have placed individuals in an assertion training group on the basis of their answers on one or two items on the scale considered together with information obtained in the interview. This may be especially true of situational nonassertive/aggressive individuals who respond unadaptively to one individual in their environment, and then only under very circumscribed situations (e.g., "I am unable to ask my boss for a raise when I think I have earned one").

Finally, keep in mind that, although there is evidence of change in both self-report measures and behavioral indices of assertiveness following assertion training, these correlations are not one-to-one (McFall & Marston, 1970; McFall & Lillesand, 1971; Friedman, 1971; Rathus, 1972; Young,

56

Rimm & Kennedy, 1973; McFall & Twentyman, 1973). Given the above limitations, we would suggest that you clarify and discuss the individual items of the questionnaires with the client, both before and after treatment, and use these paper-and-pencil measures as an adjunct to the overall screening and evaluation process.

Learning about anxiety and how to measure it

Once we believe the individual has a basic understanding of the philosophy and the principles in the assertion training process, and after we have completed the initial assessment phase, we then teach the client how to monitor and record anxiety levels. In that an integral part of assertion training involves learning how to manage unadaptive anxiety states, we believe it is important to introduce this topic early in the assertion training program. Some individuals are generally unaware of their internal states of calmness and tension, noticing the anxiety or its effects only after it reaches obviously disturbing proportions. Others believe they are anxious all of the time and can find nothing, including tranquilizers, which seems to neutralize this anxiety. In addition, there are those clients who are aware of their high levels of anxiety and who spend a great deal of time and energy trying to hide this anxiety from others.

In the second phase of the ADCP training process, we begin teaching our clients more about anxiety, how to monitor it, and how to become more aware of its parameters. We emphasize that our goal is not to eliminate the future occurrence of any anxiety in their lives. When they try out a new assertive response style, when they are in a new situation, or when they are being confronted by an angry individual, they will more than likely experience some degree of anxiety. Instead, our goal is to teach them how to recognize and neutralize some of this anxiety so it does not unadaptively interfere with what they are attempting to accomplish. In doing such, it is important that clients learn to recognize when they are just beginning to feel uncomfortable and tense. It is explained that only when their tension level is relatively low will we ask them to begin trying new assertive skills, and it is in these situations that they will most likely be able to achieve the greatest measure of success since they will more likely be able to "keep their cool" and more effectively think through and solve any problematic unexpected turn of events.

Some people are not even aware that the uncomfortable feelings they are experiencing are anxiety symptoms. We have frequently heard clients say that they believe they have a heart disease because they feel "tightness in the chest" and "heart palpitations." Others fear they have ulcers due to persistent "stomach pains," or they fear the presence of a brain tumor due to "headaches." It is important that these physical disorders be ruled out through consultation with a physician. However, once it is determined that these distress symptoms are the result of anxiety, it is important that the individual recognize these symptoms for what they are. In helping the person identify some of the individualized reactions to stress, we have found it useful to have a list of some of the more common anxiety symptoms which we show to the client. Table 4 is a modified version of a table appearing in Buss' *Psychopathology* (1966). We have changed the table somewhat by dividing the various anxiety responses into somatic and motor symptoms of anxiety and into affective and cognitive symptoms of anxiety. Under the first category, we have included symptoms that are more amenable to client observation. In the second category we have included reactions to stress that are not as directly observable and require different kinds of measurement.

Subjective Units of Discomfort Scale (SUDS)
In teaching clients to become aware of their individualized levels of calmness and tension, we utilize a measure called "SUDS." We introduce SUDS to our clients in the following manner.

SUDS is a subjective measure we constantly use in assertion training which stands for the "Subjective Units of Discomfort Scale." This scale is essentially the same as Wolpe's Subjective Units of Disturbance Scale (1969); however, we have changed the name a bit since we do

Table 4   Anxiety symptoms

Somatic and motor symptoms

Flushing	Feeling of weakness
Sweating	Intestinal distress
Dry mouth	Muscular tightness
Shallow breathing	Tremors
Chest tightness	Startle reaction
Heart palpitation	Incoordination
Pounding pulse	"Freezing" or "going blank"
Headache	

Affective and cognitive symptoms

Panic	Dread
Depression	Inattention
Irritability	Forgetfulness
Agitation	Distractibility
Worry	Nightmares

Adapted with permission from A. H. Buss. *Psychopathology.* New York: John Wiley & Sons, 1966, p. 51.

not like the connotations of the word "disturbance," and we use a scale from 0 to 100 points while Wolpe uses a 0 to 10-point scale. At any given point in time, your SUDS can range from 0 to 100, with 0 representing a state of complete calmness and relaxation, and 100 representing a state of panic.

In order to find your individual zero point on this scale, think of a situation where you have felt very relaxed and comfortable. It may be while you are sitting in a comfortable chair listening to music, taking a nice warm bath, walking on the beach (in the woods, in a meadow), meditating, just prior to falling asleep, etc. Find a situation that fits for you, and give this relaxing situation a rating of 0. Once you have a scene in mind that fits the criterion of 0 for you, then find a scene on the other end of the continuum that would produce a state of panic in you if it were to occur. Give this situation a rating of 100. At this end of the scale, it may be something like being chased by a large rabid dog, being in an elevator as the cable breaks, giving a talk before a large audience, or finding yourself locked in a dark room.

With these two situations as anchoring points, stop for a moment and determine where your SUDS measure is right now. Do not use a description such as "pretty relaxed," "bored," or "fairly uptight"; instead, give yourself a specific number which represents how you feel. Give yourself a number, and see if you can now relate this to physiological factors such as your breathing, heart rate, sweaty hands, and so forth. This is purely a subjective rating, and a 20 on your scale may mean something very different than a 20 on someone else's scale. However, this scale will allow you to tune in to your unique feeling state more accurately at any given moment, and, as such, it can be extremely valuable in determining how rapidly and in what direction the assertion training proceeds.

When we first introduce the SUDS measure, we often find that individuals will give us a range of numbers rather than a single number (e.g., 20 to 30 or about 90 to 100 instead of 25 or 99.4). When this occurs, we ask the individual to decide upon and give us a single number, indicating that the more this scale is utilized, the easier it will become to choose a specific number. A typical homework exercise for our clients in this phase of training is for them to monitor their SUDS in as many different situations as possible until they are able to discriminate and report their physical levels of calmness and tension in a systematic manner. To facilitate this learning process, we introduce the SUDS Diary.

SUDS Diary

The SUDS Diary is a record sheet used in the training of relaxation/anxiety awareness. As clients go about their daily activities between training sessions, they are asked to monitor their feelings of relaxation and anxiety and to try to place these feelings on the 100-point SUDS continuum. To facilitate this learning process, the SUDS Diary is given as a hand-out to be completed between the group sessions. On this Diary, the client is asked to identify and record a brief description of situations occurring in his life which produce different levels of relaxation and anxiety. Together with the brief description of the situation, the client is also asked to describe his physical symptoms (such as heart rate, muscle tenseness, feelings of warmth or cold) and how well he was able to think and function at the time the situation occurred. The SUDS scores are already marked on the SUDS Diary in increments of 10 points each so that the client will focus on the entire range of the 100-point scale. During the time that the client uses the Diary, he is asked to describe one situation that produced SUDS within the 0-9 range, one situation that produced SUDS within the 10-19 range, and so on. We are particularly interested in having the client learn at what levels on his subjective scale he is unable to think clearly and when he feels like running away from a situation. In that we are primarily interested in teaching the client how to tune into and record levels of relaxation/anxiety at this phase of the training program, the different situations that the client records on the SUDS Diary may or may not relate to assertion issues.

In Table 5, we have presented a completed SUDS Diary filled out by a mythical client, Pandora. Pandora filled out the SUDS Diary using some situations that did not relate to assertion. In completing the Diary, she was able to find ten situations that produced varying degrees of SUDS which ranged throughout the 100-point continuum, and she was able to identify and record several physical symptoms related to her feelings of relaxation and anxiety.

Following some practice, it is not atypical to receive a SUDS Diary as complete as Pandora's. Again, the main pur-

Table 5   Subjective Units of Discomfort (SUDS) Diary

Name _____ Pandora

Date	SUDS	Describe situation	Describe anxiety/relaxation responses
	0-9	Went sailing with my husband and oldest son	Slow breathing, calm, aware of wind on my face
	10-19	Driving on the freeway to go shopping	Normal breathing; muscles in hand, back and neck were tense
	20-29	Opened bill which I knew would be high	Slight hand shake opening envelope, stomach tight
	30-39	Phone call from high pressure salesperson; couldn't say no	Voice trembling, stomach tense, breathing faster
	40-49	Waited in line at department store 10 minutes while others cut in ahead of me	Stomach tight, back muscles tense, arms and legs slightly trembling, heart beat faster
	50-59	Stopped by police officer for speeding—got ticket	Light headed, mouth dry, sweaty palms, stammering, voice cracking
	60-69	Oldest son told me he hated me and took my car without my permission	"Tight band" feeling in head, trembling, tears in eyes, tight stomach
	70-79	Husband yelled at me for overdrawing on the checking account when it was his error	Heart beating fast, tight stomach, mind went blank, couldn't think
	80-89	Had fight with husband, told me I couldn't go to school this year	Dizzy, heart racing, crying
	90-100	Husband demanded to have sex with me when I told him I didn't feel like it	Cried, stomach tight, felt like running out of room, shaking all over

62

pose of this Diary is to help clients become more aware of their internal bodily states and how these states are affected by various situations in their lives. From the trainer's standpoint, this scale is useful as another way of becoming familiar with the client's individualized range and interpretation of the SUDS scale as well as what physical symptoms occur at the different levels of the relaxation/anxiety continuum.

Obtaining baseline data and building hierarchies
with respect to present assertion skills

In this phase of the training process, clients are taught to identify current situations in their lives that relate to assertion issues as well as to formulate goals as to how they would like to respond differently in the future. As an extension of the SUDS Diary, they are asked to monitor their SUDS and their responses in assertion-related situations. The assessment measure they use for this aspect of the assertion training process is the Assertion Training Diary (ATD). In Table 6 we have presented a completed ATD by our client, Pandora.

As indicated in the second column of the ATD, Pandora described six situations where she felt she responded in a nonassertive manner. Using the 2x2 matrix described in Chapter 2 and reproduced in Table 7, it can be seen that five of these situations occurred with a friend or intimate relationship. Furthermore, three of the situations involved making a refusal response and three of the responses involved a request. Consequently, if subsequent ATD reports showed similar patterns, we would conclude that Pandora was experiencing most of her assertion difficulties with friends and intimates in making both request and refusal responses. This information is extremely valuable not only with respect to the situations that would be discussed and role-played during the assertion training sessions, but also in respect to future homework assignments.

The SUDS rating on the ATD is designed to serve several purposes in the assertion training process. By asking individuals to monitor their anxiety level during the interaction, they must do some thinking and concentration. It has been our experience that thinking and concentration is, in

Table 6   *Assertion Training Diary*

Name _____ Pandora

Date

	Assertion-related situation	SUDS High-Low	A) What happened? and B) How did you feel?	Future goals related to this situation
	I needed to ask my neighbor-friend to baby-sit for me.	50-30	A) I asked my husband to do it for me. B) I felt helpless.	I want to be comfortable to ask myself.
	I was served a meal at a rest-aurant and it was improperly prepared.	45-20	A) I ate it like they served it. B) All I did was complain to my husband and feel upset.	I want to send the food back and get it prepared the way I like it.
	My husband demanded sex from me.	95-80	A) I ended up having sex with him. B) I felt angry and I managed to start a fight about his rela-tives later on.	I want to be able to tell him no and mean it!
	I wanted to tell my husband I wanted to go to school.	80-60	A) I sent in the application. B) I am afraid of a fight when I tell him.	I want to tell him the truth.
	I wanted to go out to eat.	45-30	A) I developed a fake headache from the heat of the kitchen. B) I felt guilty for lying.	I want to be able to refuse to cook!
	My oldest son asked to use my car.	45-20	A) I gave in to him. B) I worried about his reckless driving all night.	I don't know where to start with him!

Table 7   *Assertive response skills*

	Approach/Request	Protective/Refusal
Strangers/Situational Relationships	1. Food served improperly at a restaurant (Asking for better service)	
Friends/Intimate Relationships	1. Neighbor: Asking her to baby-sit 2. Husband: Asking him to go out to eat instead of cooking	1. Husband: Saying no to him when he asked for sex 2. Husband: Protect myself against his anger about enrolling in school 3. Son: Refuse him the use of the car

itself, a counter-conditioning agent incompatible with anxiety; consequently, the person's anxiety level will tend to be reduced if he is given a task to do during the actual interaction. Secondly, by constantly monitoring SUDS during interpersonal interactions, individuals frequently become more aware of situations where they are stuffing their emotions and doing or saying nothing about them. From the trainer's standpoint, knowing the anxiety level allows the trainer to discriminate which situations are the most difficult for that particular client. From this information, the trainer and client can then begin to establish a step-by-step hierarchy of assertion-related issues with which the client can work. For example, in Pandora's case, the first step might be to build assertive skills with individuals who did not initially create extremely high levels of anxiety and discomfort (e.g., a waitress at a restaurant). Only after she is able to report some success in handling these relationships would we specifically give her a homework assignment to be more assertive with her neighbor, son, or husband.

The fourth column of the ATD is concerned with what happened in the situation and how the person felt after the situation was over. The information supplied in this segment of the ATD is extremely helpful in both the discussion and the behavioral rehearsal aspects of assertion training. During the early stages of training, individuals sometimes indicate that they are not certain if an assertive response was called for or not in a specific situation. When such a question arises, we ask them to consider their dignity and self-worth in the situation. That is, if they felt that their dignity or self-worth was not damaged or infringed upon by responding the way they did in the situation, then, perhaps, the response was an assertive one. On the other hand, if they felt their dignity or self-worth suffered as a result of the response or lack of a response, then there is, hopefully, a better solution to be learned and practiced. Although this seemingly simple formula has been very helpful in teaching individuals what to record on their ATD, it should be kept in mind that some individuals are very naive as to their basic rights as human beings (Alberti & Emmons, 1974). Consequently, before some individuals can appropriately apply this dignity formula (Salter, 1974) to their lives, some consciousness raising and education may be needed (Phelps & Austin, 1975).

In the case of Pandora, all of the situations reported are relatively clear issues of nonassertive behavior. With her neighbor, she was not direct and had her husband speak for her; at the restaurant, she complained to her husband but said nothing to the person serving them; with her son, she gave in against her better judgment; and with her husband, she gave in with sex, avoided dealing with the school situation, and lied about cooking in order to get her way. Pandora's inability to share her feelings and make requests/refusals is a common occurrence in the lives of many nonassertive people. They tend to be secretive of their feelings and desired actions, stuff their emotions, and, as a result, often end up being misunderstood and lonely. Once these

66

feelings can be brought into the open by writing them down or through discussion, future goals can be set in order to act more assertively and reduce negative feelings.

In setting assertive goals with the individual, a considerable amount of information can be obtained from the last column of the ATD. In assessing these self-reported future goals on the ATD, time is spent discussing the realities of achieving these goals, whether the desired future behaviors seem appropriate to the situation, possible negative consequences which may occur, and intermediate steps which may be appropriate. Once this has been accomplished, some additional time is spent reducing anxiety and doing behavioral rehearsal so that these desired goals may be accomplished. With respect to the "appropriateness" of a desired goal, nonassertive individuals will sometimes describe an "aggressive" rather than an "assertive" goal in their ATD. For example, a frustrated employee who feels she is not getting paid what she deserves may indicate on the ATD that she wants to "tell her boss off" rather than learn how to ask for a raise. In the case of Pandora, rather than "refusing to cook" or "going on strike," a more appropriate first goal might be talking with her husband about wanting to eat out more often, or, possibly doing some contracting around this issue. In situations such as these, it is the therapist's job to help find assertive solutions which respect the rights and dignity of all parties concerned.

Finally, in the case of Pandora, some attempt would be made to meet with her husband and son during the course of her training. It has been our experience that if the individuals who are causing the person difficulty can be met and worked with, the training process goes much quicker and smoother. This procedure allows for all parties to be heard from, and for each to express his individual needs and goals. In these situations, we essentially attempt to teach a more open and assertive communication system between all significant parties. If the husband, for example, is just one of several individuals with whom the client is experiencing difficulty, then the husband would be seen in order to work out the assertive problems occurring between the couple, and then to provide support and encouragement to our client as she works on her assertive difficulties with others (e.g., instead of speaking for her at a restaurant to return food, he may coach and support her for her own verbal responses to the waiter). In some cases, it may not be possible to get other individuals into the training process. When this occurs, one must proceed more cautiously in that the other person's feelings and perceptions may not be represented in a fair or accurate manner.

As described in this section, the ATD can be an extremely useful tool in the third phase of the Assertive Data Collection Package. Not only does it enable the client and therapist to become more aware of the client's nonassertive/ aggressive issues, but it also enables the client and therapist to begin setting structure and formulating specific behavioral responses with which to work.

Setting treatment goals with the Assertive Goal Scale

An extension of the Assertion Training Diary (ATD) is the Assertive Goal Scale (AGS). We have designed the AGS in order to derive additional working information about specific assertive goals that the client has set for himself. More specifically, the AGS requests information on what the goal is; how long the person believes it will take to achieve this goal; one related short-range goal which produces less stress than the main goal; the anticipated SUDS in reaching these goals; and the worst possible outcome that one imagines as a result of attempting to be more assertive in this situation. In addition, the AGS allows for more than one main goal to be described, and asks for a rank ordering of these main goals in terms of their importance to the individual. As an example of how the AGS can be used with a client, we have included a partially completed AGS for Pandora in Table 8.

As can be seen in Table 8, the information supplied by Pandora on the AGS is a direct extension of the information given in her Assertion Training Diary. However with the AGS we have obtained a considerable amount of additional information regarding these two long-range goals. With respect to the initial and the final SUDS levels when achieving the desired short- and long-range goals, we can discuss if this

68

seems reasonable given the goal in question and the individual's previous SUDS responses on the SUDS Diary and on the Assertion Training Diary. If, for example, the client thought that there would be no anxiety when responding assertively to a new or difficult situation, this belief needs to be corrected and clarified.

The anticipated length of time the client feels it will take to complete the long- and short-range goals also needs to be discussed and evaluated in terms of the previous information collected. Although the anticipated time periods that Pandora has set for herself seem reasonable, it is not unusual for clients to set unrealistic goals for themselves or realistic goals to be met within unrealistic time periods. If either one of these latter situations goes uncorrected, then the client is likely to be frustrated with the assertion training experience and may even feel a sense of failure when these original expectations are not met. Consequently, by having a client specify these goals and time expectations, the danger of misunderstanding can be greatly reduced.

The client's catastrophic fantasy of asserting in a particular situation must be carefully discussed. It is at this point in the training process that many of the relationship myths are dealt with in some detail. It is also at this point that we once again carefully evaluate the potential positive versus the potential negative consequences of taking an assertive stance. If, for example, Pandora felt her friend would understand her concern if she were able to express her feelings, Pandora may feel comfortable about working on that goal at this time. On the other hand, if Pandora felt her husband was extremely unreasonable and that any resistance on her part would result in a divorce that she did not want to risk until she was able to finish her schooling, she may decide to back off of this issue for awhile and re-set her assertive goal. The important point here is that the client should make the ultimate decision as to whether these "catastrophic fantasies" are realistic, and if they are, whether one should take the risk of responding, given the present circumstances in the client's life. Our goal as assertion trainers is to teach the individual the necessary skills to make the assertive response if he

Table 8   Assertive Goal Scale

Name _____ Pandora _____   Date _____

	Goal No. 1	Goal No. 2	Goal No. 3	Goal No. 4
Describe your long-range goal.	Refuse unreasonable demands made on me by my husband (e.g., be able to say "No" to having sex when I am too tired).	Be able to ask my neighbor for baby-sitting help when my regular sitter gets sick.		
Where would you like your SUDS level to be when you achieve this goal?	15-30	10-15		
How long do you think it will take to achieve this long-range goal?	6 months	3 months		
Describe at least one short-range goal that will help you achieve your long-range goal.	Being able to say "No" to my husband when he asks me to fix fancy dinners for him on very short notice.	Be able to request that a cold meal served to me in a restaurant be sent back to the kitchen and warmed up.		

	Goal No. 1	Goal No. 2	Goal No. 3	Goal No. 4
Where would you like your SUDS level to be when you achieve this short-range goal?	15-30	5-15		
How long do you think it will take to achieve this short-range goal?	2 months	1 month		
What do you anticipate your SUDS will be when you first assert in this short-range situation?	40-75	25-50		
What is the worst possible outcome of your anxiety in this long-range goal?	He will divorce me or have an affair with some-one else.	I will make a fool of myself and forget what to say or I will lose the friendship of my neighbor.		
Number in order how important this long-range goal is in relation to the others you have listed.	1	2		

71

chooses to do so. We can give our personal opinions and we can challenge the wisdom of the individual's course of action; however, in the end, the decision to respond or not to respond based on the catastrophic fantasy appropriately lies with the individual and not with the trainer.

The final component of the AGS, the rank ordering of goals in terms of importance, permits the client to begin formulating his own hierarchy. If the SUDS values and the catastrophic fantasies were roughly equal between two or more goals, then we would begin with the goal that the client ranked as being the most important. On the other hand, if the SUDS or the catastrophic fantasy were very disproportionate, as is the case with Pandora, then we would follow a desensitization model (Wolpe, 1958, 1969) and work with the easiest goal first, gradually working up to the more difficult goals in a step-by-step manner.

Although the AGS is administered at the beginning and at the conclusion of the training program for evaluation purposes, our preference is to also administer the AGS (and, if necessary, revise the scaled goals) at periodic intervals ranging from six to twelve sessions, depending upon the individual and the goals selected. This practice of setting and revising the goals if necessary helps establish an implicit agreement between the trainer and client as to what services are being contracted and paid for in the course of therapy. In addition, the goals provide the client and trainer with an indication of what the client would like to achieve.

Practicing and monitoring
new assertive skills with the Homework Diary

The fifth and final phase of the ADCP procedure involves the client monitoring his progress as he goes through the assertion training program. As the client is taught new skills and has practiced some assertive behaviors within the training session, he is given specific between-session homework assignments to carry out and record.

Homework assignments, record keeping, and reporting are an integral part of our assertion groups as they have been for others (Salter, 1949; Wolpe & Lazarus, 1966; Lazarus, 1966; Neuman, 1969; Alberti & Emmons, 1970; Fensterheim, 1972; Booraem & Flowers, 1972; Cotler, 1973, 1975). In making these homework assignments, it is very important that they be given in a hierarchical order, with the least stressful tasks being assigned first so that the probability for success is maximized. As several investigators have previously indicated (Wolpe & Lazarus, 1966; Alberti & Emmons, 1974; Fensterheim, 1972; Cotler, 1973), if the individual's first attempts to be assertive are met with negative consequences, he is much less likely to try out different assertive behaviors later on.

In keeping a record of their homework assignments, clients are asked to complete a Homework Diary sheet. On this Diary, the client is asked what the specific assignment was, his SUDS in completing the assignment, what he did, how successful he felt in completing the assignment, and what future goals or suggestions for improvement he may have as a result of this assignment. In Table 9 we have presented a completed Homework Diary for Pandora where her assignments were directly related to the information obtained in the previous measures of the ADCP. Also, as indicated in the second assignment she completed, there is room for input and flexibility on the part of the client in completing these homework assignments.

The material described in the client's Homework Diary constitutes many of the situations that are discussed, role-played, and coached during the sessions. They later serve as one means of evaluating the success of the assertion training process. We have introduced the topic of homework assignments and the Homework Diary here because this is one aspect of the ADCP. However, the major emphasis on homework assignments comes later in the assertion training process (see Chapter 11).

Relaxation training

The purpose of relaxation training is to enable the individual to reduce his feelings of "tension" and "anxiety" (we use the words "tension," "anxiety," and "discomfort" simultaneously under the label of "SUDS"), which often interfere with responding in an assertive manner. Relaxation, like

Table 9   Homework Diary

Name _____ Pandora

Date	Homework assignment	SUDS High-Low	What did you do?	Evaluate your success in completing assignment 0 (none) 5 (moderate) 10 (completely successful)	Future goals
9-15	Call the information operator and ask for an out-of-state phone number.	30-20	Forgot city in which person lived at first. Felt my hands sweating a bit.	5	Be able to do this with less anxiety.
9-16	Decided on my own to repeat yesterday's assignment three more times today.	25-10	I became more comfortable at this each time. SUDS was at 10 on third try.	9	Be able to ask operator to repeat number twice without increasing my SUDS.
9-17	Return item to a store.	55-25	Clerk said store policy was no refunds. Gave me an exchange slip but would not refund my money.	4	Would like to be able to return items and get a cash refund without feeling too anxious.
9-18	Talk to a neighbor about baby-sitting situation, but not make a specific request at this time.	40-30	Brought subject into ongoing topic of conversation. Neighbor volunteered to help me without my asking.	10	Be more open with my neighbor—she really understood my problem and was super kind.
9-19	Go to restaurant and order one type of salad dressing and then change dressing order before waitress leaves table.	35-20	Went OK, voice cracked a bit, but I was still able to change order.	7	Be able to do this when someone else is with me at the restaurant.

assertion, is a skill. As such, it can be taught to others in a systematic fashion. Relaxation training has been shown to be useful not only as part of systematic desensitization in reducing intense fears (Wolpe, 1958, 1969) but also as a procedure in itself for treating problems such as generalized anxiety, insomnia, high blood pressure, tachycardia, and headaches.

Relaxation training requires some regular home practice if it is going to be useful in helping to alleviate anxiety at a later time. Some clients have the tendency to practice the relaxation only if they are in group, are feeling really good, or are in the midst of an anxiety attack. For relaxation training to be useful, it needs to be practiced on a more regular basis, and this practice needs to be monitored and reinforced periodically by the therapist.

The type of relaxation training that we generally use is divided into two phases (Cotler & Guerra, 1975). The first relaxation session is spent teaching the client an abbreviated form of Jacobson's (1938) progressive relaxation whereby the client tenses and then relaxes various muscle groups of the body from the toes to the head. The purpose of this treatment phase is to teach the individual how to differentiate between a state of tension and a state of relaxation. It has not been uncommon to find individuals who report a high level of tension and yet are unaware of the locus of this tension or how pervasive it is throughout the body.

It has also been our experience that individuals are most often aware of their anxiety only at the higher ranges. By this time, the ability to appropriately handle the situation and quickly reduce the tension is greatly diminished. An individual with very high levels of anxiety does not have full access to his best reasoning powers, and the incoming information is often distorted. By becoming aware of low levels of anxiety before it gets out of hand, one can often initiate some relaxation procedures to prevent higher levels of anxiety and perceptual distortion from occurring. By going through these tension-relaxation exercises, the client is much better able to identify and localize feelings of tension and anxiety when they first begin to appear. Specific procedural steps for going through these tension-relaxation exercises can be found in Wolpe & Lazarus (1966), Bernstein & Borkovec (1973) and Cotler & Guerra (1975).

The next phase of training involves giving the client practice in visualizing scenes that are intended to elicit feelings of relaxation. Before beginning the visualization practice, the client is asked to describe situations where he is able to relax and acquire a sense of inner calmness (i.e., a very low SUDS). Typical scenes are walking along or lying on the beach, taking a nice warm bath, walking through the woods or a meadow, listening to music while sitting in a comfortable chair, watching the sun go down in a picturesque part of the world, lying in a warm bed, or getting a body massage.

At times, when the client cannot think of any relaxing scenes, you may want to utilize situations that make *you* feel relaxed and at peace with yourself; however, make certain afterwards that the scenes you chose were, in fact, relaxing for the client. One of our clients became very upset when given the scene of relaxing on a beach—it was soon discovered that the client had a phobia of beaches since landing on Iwo Jima during World War II.

During this second phase of training, the client is asked to close his eyes while the therapist describes four to six relaxing scenes in as much detail as possible. In between the presentation of these scenes, the client is given some additional tasks such as counting backwards slowly, instructions for deep breathing, and rating his SUDS at given points.

Both the first and the second sessions of the relaxation training procedure (i.e., the muscle tension-relaxation and the visualization of scenes) have been recorded on cassette tapes (Cotler & Guerra, 1975). The client is asked to practice these relaxation procedures daily for fifteen to thirty minutes at home in a setting free of interruptions and noise. At first, the client is instructed to use the tapes as a guide to follow. After the client becomes familiar with the sequence on the tape, he is then instructed to go through the procedure without the tape, moving at an individualized pace and assuming increasingly more responsibility for the relaxation.

Generally within three to six weeks, we find that individuals are able to appreciably reduce their feelings of tension within short periods of time by just saying the word "relax," by visualizing one or two of the relaxing scenes, or by slowly counting backward from ten to zero while breathing comfortably. When the relaxation training is presented as part of the group process, it is usually done during the last half hour of the early group sessions. In later sessions throughout the therapy, the last ten minutes are occasionally devoted to group relaxation practice.

During all phases of relaxation training, the client is encouraged to practice deep, comfortable breathing from the diaphragm. When individuals become tense, they often begin breathing in a rapid and shallow manner. By just having the individual stop what he is doing, take a couple of deep breaths, and say the word "relax" to himself, we find that his anxiety will drop considerably. We, therefore, use this procedure frequently during the behavioral rehearsal phase of treatment in order to reduce the individual's SUDS and to give him some additional thinking time before having to respond. On several occasions we have been told that the ability to relax is one of the first behaviors that clients begin using in their outside environments. As such, relaxation can be very important to the application and generalization of simultaneously learned assertive behaviors.

6 Setting up
an assertion training group

In setting up an assertion training group, the therapist must consider a number of interrelated issues. Among these issues are the size and composition of the group, the number of therapists involved and how they are selected, the length of the training sessions, and the length of the group program itself.

The advantages of group training

Although assertion training procedures were originally discussed as a one-to-one therapy procedure (Salter, 1949; Wolpe, 1958), increasingly more attention has been given to the use and value of assertion groups (Lazarus, 1968; Lomont et al., 1969; Hedquist & Weinhold, 1970; Alberti & Emmons, 1970, 1974; Fensterheim, 1972; Booraem & Flowers, 1972; Bloomfield, 1973; Cotler, 1973, 1975; Flowers & Guerra, 1974; Shoemaker & Paulson, 1973). This interest in assertion groups is well justified for several reasons. One reason relates to the use of *behavioral rehearsal* in assertion training whereby the individual repeatedly practices by role-playing (under the direct supervision and direction of the therapist) those social or interpersonal situations which are causing him difficulty until he is able to replace these deficient behaviors with more effective and efficient behavior patterns (Lazarus, 1968; McFall & Lillesand, 1971).

In a one-to-one therapy situation, the therapist must play the role of the boss, the spouse, the parent, or the friend with whom the client is having difficulty and, at the same time, "coach" the client as to alternative and more assertive response styles. In some cases, this can become an extremely difficult juggling act. For one, the therapist may be put into a position where he is playing several roles almost simultaneously. Secondly, the client may experience high levels of anxiety with which the therapist must contend. This may be due to the situation itself, the therapist's "authority" position, or because the therapist possesses certain characteristics that resemble the client's boss, spouse, or friend. However, in a group situation, another client or co-therapist who elicits lower levels of anxiety for the client can initially play the role of the "significant other," leaving the therapist free to coach the client and tune in to the client's SUDS and behaviors. From the client's standpoint, this process can be extremely useful in two ways: It gives the individual who is learning assertive behaviors the opportunity to work with people of different sexes, ages, backgrounds, and ways of relating, and it gives the other group members the opportunity to practice and understand the different roles of an assertive interaction. Our experience has been that individuals seem much more open to changing their response styles after they have had the opportunity to be both the assertor and the recipient of an assertive interaction.

Also, by conducting assertion training in groups, it is possible to gradually train other group members to take over the role of coach and therapist. As Flowers & Guerra (1974) have reported, individuals who had the opportunity to serve as a "coach" learned assertive behaviors better than those who do not get this practice as part of their training.

Another advantage of the group model is that a wide variety of assertive, nonassertive, and aggressive responses are reported by the different group members—more than are apt to be introduced by a single therapist or client. By constantly working with a broad range of situations, the client is usually able to see applications of assertive behaviors far beyond what he might have originally imagined. Likewise, in that there may be several assertive ways of dealing with any particular situation, the client is able through behavioral rehearsal and discussion to see a number of possible assertive solutions to a problem. Also, because we place nonassertive and aggressive clients in the same group, the individual is more likely to observe the extremes of behavior displayed by others. Consequently, the client can more easily discover the assertive "middle ground" between nonassertion and aggression.

Finally, clients in assertion training tend to give one another a great deal of support and feedback as progress is being made and as new response styles are being learned. Consequently, a considerable amount of *esprit de corps* can be built up in an assertion training group, and this can be extremely useful to the final outcome of training as well as during the ongoing training process.

Because of these advantages of assertion groups, we tend to utilize the group modality in most of the work we do with nonassertive/aggressive individuals.

Moving from individual to group sessions

Often the therapist is confronted with an individual who he feels would benefit from some assertion training, but who is initially much too anxious to be put into any type of group situation. Under these circumstances, we often see the individual on a one-to-one basis until his anxiety level is sufficiently reduced or until his skill level is sufficiently improved to handle the group process. During this time, we may attempt to reduce the anticipatory anxiety of being in a group through the use of systematic desensitization (Wolpe, 1958, 1969), by teaching the person some "protective skills" so that he can feel some "control" over what happens to him in the group, and by stressing the fact that the trainers will be supportive of the individual in the group and will attempt to minimize any confrontation, anxiety, or high levels of stress.

When we do make the transfer into the group process with those individuals who are initially very anxious, we have found it to be very desirable to allow the new member to just sit in the group for one to three sessions without expecting him to do more than observe the group process. In such cases, the person does not have to say anything about himself or answer any questions unless he wants to do so. At the same time, he can ask questions or make comments to others in the group who are not there under similar contingencies. The other group members are informed of this situation and tend not to exert any pressure on the individual—if they do, the trainer immediately comes to the aid of the new member. We have found this procedure very effective in shaping a group-anxious individual into the group process, and, as yet, we have not had any individuals drop from group because of their initial group phobic behavior.

One must be aware that anxious, nonassertive clients may wish to sit in a group for months without saying much. Consequently, our early sessions with these individuals are structured so that in each session they are asked to talk and interact a little more according to a predetermined and mutually agreed upon hierarchy. For example, during the first session, the client may only be required to say his name. In the second session, he may be asked to share some personal self-disclosure such as his occupation, marital status, or hobbies. In the third session, the client may be asked to share with the other group members some of his assertion difficulties and goals. In this manner, the client is gradually shaped into becoming more active and comfortable with the ongoing group process.

Size and composition of the group

Most of our assertion training groups are composed of eight to twelve members. This includes six to ten clients, two or three therapists, and sometimes one visitor during each session. There is no magic formula for deriving this "eight to twelve" figure, and, in part, it has been determined by the size of our office space. In the past, we have run assertion groups with as few as three clients and as many as thirty-five clients; however, we would generally recommend a total of no fewer than six and no more than fifteen individuals.

Whereas the clients in our groups are, for the most part, roughly similar with respect to their lack of psychoses and low dependency on phenothiazine-type drugs, there are broad variations with respect to the degree to which they are limited in their nonassertive/aggressive behaviors, their socio-

82

economic status, education, age, occupation, marital status, and sex. Although this group composition is different from some of the groups that others have described (Lazarus, 1968; Fensterheim, 1972; Shoemaker & Paulson, 1973), we have found this heterogeneity of group membership to be extremely valuable in the behavioral rehearsal phase of assertion training. By having a broad spectrum of individuals present, it is much easier to set up a hierarchy so that the client begins practicing his assertive skills through role-playing with someone who elicits a tolerable amount of anxiety, gradually working up to those individuals in the group (whether they be another client or one of the therapists) who elicit greater levels of anxiety. Obviously, the individual whom the client may choose to begin practicing the art of a good conversation with may be quite different from the person he would put at the top of his hierarchy for working out a compromise with an "authority figure."

We have also found it beneficial, whenever possible, to have clients from both ends of the nonassertive/aggressive continuum present in the same group, especially since many of the individuals who are labeled, or label themselves, "aggressive" are actually nonassertive a good deal of the time. By having both ends of the continuum present in the same group, the clients seem to be better able to find the anchoring points and the assertive "middle ground" between *being taken advantage of by* others and *taking advantage of* others.

Multiple therapists

We have found that having at least two trained therapists present at any given time offers a distinct advantage over the single therapist model. To begin with, assertion training tends to be a very active and potentially draining experience for the therapist. Consequently, an additional therapist (or two) allows for time to just sit back and observe the group process. In addition, the coaching and behavioral rehearsal aspects of assertion training function much more smoothly and effectively with two or more therapists present in that this allows for multiple coaching to take place simultaneously. For instance, the group member with whom the "assertor" is practicing may also need help in the role-playing and in keeping his anxiety level down. Also, in the later stages of training when the larger group is broken down into smaller practice groups of two or three people, it is possible to circulate and observe these smaller groups more closely if more than one therapist is present. Finally, individual therapists often rely on different assertive response styles in dealing with the same kind of situation. Consequently, by having more than one therapist present to model how he would handle the situation, the participants have the opportunity to view alternative ways of dealing with the same situation. This seems highly desirable since individuals often find one assertive mode of responding much more comfortable and natural for them to adopt than another. The only disadvantages we have found with using two or more therapists is that the time of two or more professionals is tied up, and the fees from therapy must be divided among more people. Thus far, however, we have found that the advantages in working with another therapist (or with two other therapists) more than offset the disadvantages.

In selecting a co-therapist several criteria should be considered. First of all, and perhaps most importantly, your co-therapist should be someone you enjoy and respect as a friend as well as a fellow professional. Our experience has been that your co-therapist should not only be someone with whom you share similar therapy goals, but also someone you can easily talk with, tease, disagree with and, in general, have a good time, both during and outside of the sessions. In our opinion, some of our most meaningful and helpful teaching has occurred when we have been able to joke with one another as well as resolve some of our personal differences in front of the other group members. Some therapists may take issue with the idea of disagreeing on procedure in front of the group members. However, it is our intent to establish the therapist as a real person and not as an all-knowing, unapproachable individual who is never capable of making a mistake. Not only do we express our disagreements with one another from time to time, but we also encourage our clients to disagree (and joke) with us if they feel inclined to do so. It is important to us that clients recognize they have a right to their dignity, value systems, and opinions—with their therapists as well as the people they interact with outside of the group.

Secondly, since each therapist serves as an extremely important model to the group members, your co-therapist, like yourself, should be basically assertive in his daily activities. It may not be necessary that each co-therapist has the same extensive background in learning theory, however, the more that each of you know in this area and about other treatment modalities as well, the more stimulating and enriching the group process can be.

In that the therapist must be ultimately responsible for being able to act out the several different roles during the behavioral rehearsal aspect of treatment, each co-therapist should be flexible, creative, enthusiastic, innovative, able to play a number of different roles, and willing to experiment. Although most groups have group members who turn out to be good actors and actresses, you cannot be certain of this occurring, and, in many cases, their acting skills are not apparent until therapy has progressed to the point where their anxiety is sufficiently reduced.

It is a definite advantage, in our opinion, to have at least one male and one female co-therapist. More and more we are finding that it is, perhaps, presumptuous for a male therapist to assume that he can fully understand the nonassertive/aggressive feelings of a woman or for a woman therapist to think she can fully understand the nonassertive/aggressive feelings of a male. Consequently, by having both a male and a female therapist present, we feel you are most likely to elicit somewhat various and perhaps broader issues of assertion. (We recognize that just being male or female does not *guarantee* any special level of awareness or understanding.) Also, it may be advantageous to have a co-therapist of a specific ethnic or minority group present if this is a factor in the composition of the group.

Visitors
The visitor present at any given time can be a professional, an individual who is interested in learning more

about assertion training, or a former group member who stops by to relate how things have been going or who wants to work briefly on a particular problem. This occasional visit from a former group member, especially one who is enthusiastic and verbal about his accomplishments with assertion, can be extremely helpful and encouraging to the present group members, some of whom may be having difficulty seeing any possibilities for change. Often this visitor, whether he is another therapist or a former client, can teach the group (and the therapists) new ways of responding assertively.

We have also invited into the group on occasion an individual who is skilled in another area (e.g., drama, body awareness). We have tried to integrate this person's expertise with our own.

Permission for having a visitor join the group is first obtained from the group members, and it is understood that visitors, unlike anxious new group members, can be asked any question and asked to participate in the various procedures we practice.

Time-limited versus open-ended groups

In most cases our assertion groups meet on a weekly basis for two hours each session. We have tried meeting for shorter periods of time (one to one-and-a-half hours) and for longer periods of time (three hours); however, the two-hour time block best fits our particular training needs as well as our energy level. On a one-to-one basis, the sessions typically last one hour; however, this too may vary somewhat depending upon the issues that are being dealt with.

In terms of the length of treatment, the group can be time-limited, with a fixed number of sessions and no new members admitted after the second or third session, or open-ended with no predetermined number of sessions and with new members continually coming into the group and other members "graduating" from the group as their treatment goals have been achieved. We have found that there are advantages to each of these approaches, and choosing a time-limited versus an open-ended group depends largely upon the preferences of the therapists and on other limiting circumstances. For a group in a university setting where the clients' therapy time is somewhat dictated by a semester schedule, it may be simpler to run the group on a time-limited basis. Also, with a time-limited group it is sometimes easier to present the assertion material in a systematic manner, to collect data, and to do research because all members start and finish at the same time and practice similar procedures simultaneously. Another point to consider is the motivation level of the client. Although we have no research data as yet to support this hypothesis, it appears that some clients seem to work harder in assertion therapy when they know that there is only a fixed number of sessions to accomplish their goals. In private practice where you would not want to terminate the client if his goals have not yet been achieved in the time-limited period, there is a possibility that the client can continue in a different group or in one-to-one therapy.

With the open-ended group, certain procedures may need to be repeated at several points throughout the group as new members enter. However, this repetition may be valuable for the "older" members since they then have the opportunity to overlearn these skills, and they can serve as teachers for the newer members.

An evaluation of progress is made every eight to twelve weeks in the open-ended groups. This can be done in cooperation with the client using the Assertive Goal Scale and the Homework Diary, or it can be accomplished by a discussion or observation period in the case of a hospitalized population. During the evaluation period, the clients and trainers discuss what changes have occurred and what new short- and long-range goals are now appropriate. During these "stop, look, and decide" periods, decisions are made to terminate or "graduate" certain group members and to add others to the group.

In the course of the past four years, we have run both time-limited groups (six to twelve sessions) and open-ended groups (lasting over one year). Neither group model has emerged as the best treatment approach for all situations. In some situations, the decision to run a time-limited versus an open-ended group may be influenced by the relative homogeneity of the clients. For example, with a group of college students all working on socialization skills with members of the opposite sex, a time-limited group may be more appropriate. However, an open-ended group may be more appropriate in a situation where the training goals are very different and there are large differences in age, socioeconomic class, and occupations.

We have also found that placing a generally nonassertive individual who has many different assertion difficulties and anxieties in a time-limited group will tend to discourage him in that there seems to be "so little time to work on so many problems." Since a sense of being overwhelmed is not one of the feelings we wish to promote in our clients, we tend to refer this individual to an open-ended group with the instructions to work on one problem at a time, and we also monitor his progress every six to twelve weeks. Individuals then do not report feeling as pressured in eventually reaching their assertive goals.

Individual assertion training

There are situations where it seems best to utilize one-to-one assertion training from the beginning to the end of the training process. Naturally, if there are no groups available at the time, or if a time-limited group has gotten too far underway to transfer a client into this setting, we will work with the person individually. In other cases, one-to-one assertion training may be the treatment of choice when the identified problem is so specific and so situational that the client's time and efforts can be more efficiently spent working on a one-to-one basis (e.g., dealing with a specific person around a specific problem).

These specific situational assertion difficulties may occur, for instance, with clients who are seeing you for problems other than their lack of assertiveness alone. For example, a couple may seek your help for some marital counseling and, during the course of treatment, you may find that some, but not all, of the existing tension in the relationship is directly related to the father's inability to set limits and say

"No" to his child's demands. In this situation, the therapist must decide whether the problem is generalized enough to help the nonassertive father via an assertion group or to work with the situation in the context of the existing counseling sessions. There are no absolute answers to this type of situation, and the guidelines we use in making a decision are based upon the extent and the severity of the problem as well as on the anticipated ease of working with this particular person in a group versus a more individualized setting. If a one-to-one approach is chosen, the therapist must be fairly certain that the dimensions of the problem are understood and that the therapist will be able to effectively role-play the "significant other" in the client's environment. In the case with the couple, if both partners were supportive of each other around this issue, and if both would be willing to role-play and practice the situation while the therapist coached and trained the non-assertive father, then an assertion group may not be necessary. However, if such were not possible, or if the individualized training was going slowly with too much time being taken away from the couple's other problems, then a group training experience together with the couple counseling would be in order.

Getting referrals from other therapists

Whereas some practitioners find procedures used in assertion training very compatible with their own therapy approach and, consequently, use some of these procedures in working with their clients—it does not matter whether they call themselves "behaviorists" or not—others see the value for some assertion training but do not feel comfortable or competent enough to use these procedures. In the latter case, the therapist may wish to refer the client to someone else doing assertion training so that a specific behavioral deficiency or high interpersonal anxiety reaction can be changed. In most instances, the individual can be engaged in assertion training at the same time he is involved with a different type of therapy process with no unfavorable consequences if some ongoing contact with the referring therapist is maintained. The one complication we have observed by combining two therapy approaches simultaneously is that clients in assertion training tend to become more outspoken with respect to their needs. If they feel that their therapy needs are not being met, they tend to say so to their therapist, and, as a result, the referring therapist who is still working with the client may interpret this as "resistance" or may feel that the client is now uncooperative or unmotivated. If this problem cannot be adequately dealt with through communication with the referring therapist, it may be necessary for the client to consider taking a break from his previous therapy until the assertive issues can be resolved, at which point the client can evaluate his future therapy needs.

7 Behavioral rehearsal and coaching

Behavioral rehearsal is one of the basic components of assertion training. It essentially involves the role-playing of an experienced or anticipated situation in the individual's life that has created or is expected to create some difficulties. The client role-plays the situation while the therapist and other group members take on the roles of the coach and the "significant others." The behavioral rehearsal procedure is a combination of *in vivo* desensitization and skill training, both of which are important components of assertion training. By actively role-playing those situations which the client has avoided or which he fears, the client is, hopefully, able to acquire additional verbal and nonverbal skills and is able to reduce his anxiety level in the process.

Even though this is only a role-playing situation, we have found that a considerable amount of emotion can still be generated by this process. For example, in rehearsing a party scene where a client is having difficulty starting and maintaining conversations, the individual must actually approach someone in the group and begin talking as if he were at a party. Just thinking about this situation will usually generate some anxiety and discomfort for the individual experiencing problems in this area. The additional requirement of having to role-play this situation places the individual in the position where he must now respond with various behaviors that may have been repeatedly avoided in the past. In utilizing behavioral rehearsal, the individual is requested to practice the situation until the appropriate skills have been acquired and until the anxiety level is within tolerable limits. During this practice, the client is provided with a coach who assists the client if he gets stuck or becomes overly anxious. In addition, the situation is broken down into least stressful to most stressful components; consequently, the same situation may be rehearsed a number of times before the individual is able to get through the entire sequence with some proficiency. In cases where the individual's anxiety is initially very high, it is helpful if the client can observe someone else playing his role in a specific situation so that he can observe and vicariously experience the assertive interaction.

Setting up the rehearsal:
 Assertor, recipient, and coach

In this behavioral rehearsal procedure, the group members carry out three different role functions. The first role has already been described, and this is the role of the assertor. This is the individual who is attempting to improve or acquire a new skill and/or reduce his anxiety level. The second role is that of the *recipient* or protagonist for the assertor (i.e., the "significant other"). This individual may be another group member or one of the therapists. The recipient plays the role of the individual with whom the client has difficulty being assertive. That is, the recipient may play the role of a boss, spouse, stranger, friend, or salesperson. The sex of the recipient need not be the same as the sex of the significant other in the client's life. If the assertor is having difficulty with his wife nagging him, the initial role rehearsals may use a male playing the role of the wife if, in fact, this person generates low anxiety for the client. For example, in the following case where Joe is the assertor and Ed is playing the role of Joe's wife (the recipient), Ed would say the same words that the assertor's wife might say; however, the sex casting would be different:

Joe: Hi, honey, how was your day today?

Ed: It's about time you are home. The kids have been driving me crazy, and you didn't take out the garbage this morning before you left.

92

Joe: It sounds as if you had a bad day. But I really do not like to be screamed at the moment I walk in the door. Let's sit down and talk about the situation so that things might go better for both of us in the future.

Some interactions can be quite unrealistic, such as a twenty-three-year-old female playing the father of a thirty-year-old man, or a middle-aged woman playing the role of a burly policeman. These inconsistencies between role-playing and reality are desirable at certain stages because they provide the opportunity for using an *in vivo* desensitization with an element of humor. In most instances, the assertor is asked to rank order the group members on a continuum ranging from the person who would generate the least anxiety to the person in the room who would generate the most anxiety in this situation; the person need not indicate what criteria are used to make this ranking. Once this continuum is established, the assertor then begins his rehearsal with the group member chosen who gives the least amount of anxiety. This rehearsal continues until the assertor reports a significant reduction of anxiety. Typically, when the assertor reports a SUDS level of 10-15 with one recipient, he then continues on to the next individual he has chosen until the assertor is able to deal with anyone in the room in this particular situation.

The third role in the behavioral rehearsal is the role of the *coach.* In conducting assertion training workshops for other professionals, we have found that teaching professionals how to coach others is extremely important. On several occasions, we have set up mini-groups to teach coaches how to coach clients.

Coaching

There are three primary functions to play as a coach. These are: (1) utilizing the Subjective Units of Discomfort Scale (SUDS) with the assertor, (2) giving constant feedback and judicious positive reinforcement to the assertor, and (3) prompting and aiding the assertor when he encounters difficulties.

93

Utilizing the Subjective Units
of Discomfort Scale (SUDS)

Throughout this book we have stated the need for people to lower their inappropriate social anxieties. We have explained the SUDS scale and have described how this scale can be used to help construct a problem hierarchy for the assertor. During the behavioral rehearsal procedure, the client and the coach are in constant communication regarding the assertor's SUDS level. The SUDS level is used as a measure of the development of the ongoing role-playing process, and it allows the coach to direct the pace of the role-playing. If the rehearsal has continued for four or five minutes and the assertor's SUDS remains very high or rises sharply from the initial level, then something is wrong. If this occurs, the rehearsal should be stopped, the SUDS lowered, and the client questioned as to what is happening.

It may be that the hierarchy needs to be modified and broken down into less stressful components, the "protagonist" needs to change or be instructed to act differently, or that the pace of the interaction needs to be slowed down. In most cases, if the situation is set up carefully from the start, the SUDS will rise a bit initially and then gradually start dropping throughout the rehearsal period. With the use of the SUDS level as an indicator of anxiety, the coach can decide when to stop or how long to continue the assertor's rehearsal period. If the SUDS level of the assertor drops to levels below 10 or 15 and stays there for awhile, the coach will generally stop the interaction and either allow a rest and discussion period, set up the next rehearsal on the assertor's hierarchy, or go on to another client.

In addition to using the SUDS level as an indicator of change in the rehearsal, the coach asks the assertor to give his present SUDS level in order to interrupt and interfere with the assertor's anxiety. That is, the assertor is required to momentarily distract himself from the scene he is practicing. He thinks about the anxiety level, decides on a single number, and then communicates it to the coach. The rationale for this is that thinking is incompatible with anxiety. If the client must think and decide what his SUDS level is, then the anxiety level will tend to be lowered in the process. The SUDS level communication between assertor and coach is extremely brief. The assertor is instructed not to discuss or even look towards the coach (Co) when being asked for a SUDS rating. The assertor (As) is simply asked to pause, think, decide on a single number, say that number indicating his SUDS level, and then continue the rehearsal.

As: (Speaking to the recipient) Waitress, may I see you for a moment please?

Co: SUDS?

As: 15.

Co: Good, continue.

As: (To the recipient) My steak is too rare. I would appreciate it if you would take it back and have it cooked a little more.

In coaching, both the assertor's and the recipient's SUDS levels must be monitored if both of these individuals are clients. If the recipient has no difficulty with the rehearsal scene, then less attention needs to be given to the recipient's SUDS. However, if both the assertor and the recipient are reporting high SUDS during the behavioral rehearsal, then the coach must monitor both individuals simultaneously, or, as occurs in our groups, someone else begins serving as the coach for the recipient.

It is important that the coach be sensitive to any cues, verbal and nonverbal, which might suggest that the reported SUDS of the assertor is not an accurate indicator of his anxiety level. Discrepancies sometimes exist between what the individual reports and what the coach is observing. When this occurs, it is recommended that the process be interrupted and the coach's (Co) observations be checked out with the assertor (As).

As: Jessie, I have worked here now for three years with only a cost of living increase. Based upon the money I have generated for the company these past three years, I really believe I am due for a raise at this point.

Co: Good statement. What is your SUDS right now?

As: 15.

Co: Fifteen sounds like a very low number since your hands are shaking a bit now and your forehead is perspiring. What has been the low and high range of your SUDS since coming into this group?

As: From about 3 to 80.

Co: Given that range, do you still feel your SUDS is at 15 right now?

As: Well, it is a lot lower than I thought it would be when asking Jessie for a raise, but now that you mention it, I am not nearly as relaxed as when we did the relaxation training the other week. I think maybe 40 is a more accurate number.

If, in the above interaction, the client still held to a SUDS of 15, the coach might openly disagree with what the client reported or the coach might let the matter slide, making a mental note of the discrepancy between what the client reported and the physiological signs that were observed. As the training continued, hopefully there would be a closer correspondence between self-report measures, physiological changes, and behaviors.

Giving positive feedback to the assertor
Another role function of the coach is to give the assertor frequent, positive feedback during the behavioral rehearsal. Many of the errors made by novice coaches are in this area of insufficient feedback and support. The role of the coach is an extremely active one. The coach will not be effective if he sits idly by and just watches. Instead, both verbal and nonverbal feedback (e.g., head-nodding, smiling, touching) must be constantly given to the client. We sometimes see the coach sitting quietly *behind* the assertor, smiling and nodding his head. Although this nonverbal approval is encouraged, it does no good if the client cannot see this approval! Consequently, sit off to the side or in front of the assertor so that your nonverbal communications can be

observed. Also, remember that the assertor may be experiencing high levels of anxiety and that his discrimination abilities may not be that sharp. Therefore, it may be advisable to exaggerate some of these feedback messages to ensure that they are received by the client.

The feedback given to the client can be both verbal and nonverbal, and it need not interrupt the ongoing role-playing. The verbal statements given do not have to be long or elaborate sentences. A "good," "fine," "that's right," "far out," or "you've got it," is sufficient. In addition to the verbal responses and the head-nodding and smiling, we feel very strongly that touching is an essential element in nonverbal, positive feedback. Most people like to be touched. For a coach to say "good" and put his hand on the assertor's shoulder is, in our opinion, a very appropriate "warm fuzzy." We are in no way proposing extensive intimate physical contact between coaches and assertors. However, we do encourage parents and teachers to touch children, we encourage mates to touch each other when communicating, and we are now encouraging coaches to touch assertors—frequently. Above all, we feel that the reinforcer that is being given to the assertor needs to be honest, real, and given in a mutually comfortable manner. If you are not comfortable touching clients, or if you are not comfortable touching a particular client, then do not do it. If, by chance, you are also uncomfortable giving verbal positive feedback, then don't do it—but please don't run assertion training groups!

Prompting

The third and possibly most difficult function of the coach is *prompting*. The coach, in fulfilling this function, is required to covertly put himself in the interaction between the assertor and recipient. The coach must primarily identify with the assertor and think what he would be saying if he were actually acting assertively in this interaction. In this way the coach is prepared to give the assertor the exact words to say if the assertor gets stuck and cannot think of what to say next. In the initial stages of practice, the coach may be providing all of the words for the assertor. The coach follows the interaction, and if the assertor hesitates, then the coach says

97

a sentence that fits into the context of the conversation. The assertor may then repeat the sentence word for word, or may change it to fit his own personal style.

In this situation, the coach is attempting to serve as a social role model and, at the same time, trying to put himself in the assertor's place and come up with a response that is both appropriate and comfortable for the client. However, the reality is that the coach is drawing on his *own* feelings and values and then suggesting them as an alternative to the client. As psychotherapists, we have sometimes heard that it is not proper to do this, and that giving the client your own ways of coping with a problem is inappropriate. We disagree. We purposely intend to influence our clients. We want to sell them the assertion philosophy of equal human worth, and we want to act as social role models, hoping that some of our own assertiveness will rub off on the individuals. We are not attempting to force our clients to respond exactly as we do. However, we do present our own assertive styles and then work with the client in order to find the skills that "fit" or are comfortable for him as an individual. Other group members are also encouraged to state how they would handle any specific situation. In this way the assertor is provided with a number of different styles to observe, model, and use in developing a unique and individualized assertive response style.

As important as it is to prompt, it is equally important to know when not to prompt. A coach should assist by prompting only if the client needs it. Likewise, the coach should reinforce the individual when he is asserting in his own style. When the person begins solving his difficulties in his own way, then the coach should back off from the prompting. In doing this, wait for a three- or four-second hesitation on the assertor's part before you give a prompt. When the assertor starts to ad-lib his own responses in an interaction, you can then begin to fade your prompting. That is, if you, as a coach, give a prompt and your assertor does not repeat it word for word but changes the sentence and still asserts appropriately, you should begin to reinforce his individual style more and prompt less.

As the assertor requires progressively less attention from the coach, the recipient of the assertive interaction may also request less prompting as he gets into role-playing a particular individual in the assertor's life. Typically, some initial instructions are given to the recipient as to how the role is to be played in order to give the assertor practice in responding assertively and without producing an extremely high anxiety state. However, even with these preparatory comments, the recipient will occasionally push the assertor beyond the limits which he can handle at that point. When this occurs, the coach must quickly step in and direct the interaction towards a successful conclusion for the *assertor*.

To summarize, the coach must watch both the assertor and the recipient for high SUDS. If the anxiety becomes too high, an effort must be made to lower it. The coach should also give constant feedback and support. In addition, the coach must be prepared to give prompting on a moment's notice if necessary. Finally, the coach must know when to back off, when to allow an interaction to continue, and when to redirect or halt the interaction. The coaching role is an active and difficult function to fill. Consequently, we strongly encourage you to get some training experience in coaching and to use multiple trainers when first learning these skills.

Additional aids to behavioral rehearsal

Overlearning skills and spontaneous recovery

As a matter of standard practice in the behavioral rehearsal experiences, the assertor overlearns the skill that he is working on. This overlearning process involves repeated role-playing experience with a specific situation until the assertive responses become almost automatic and the anxiety level is well within tolerable limits. When a client reports that, "I am bored with this; I want to move on," we as assertion trainers are happy. It is not that we enjoy boring our clients, but rather, people are not usually bored with a frightening situation. When a client reports boredom, he is essentially stating that he is no longer anxious. With practice, we feel that when the individual faces an assertive situation in his real environment, he will be able to handle the situation better than if the practice did not occur.

We have clients overlearn their skills for two basic reasons. To begin with, there is the process of *spontaneous recovery*. Spontaneous recovery is the reoccurrence of a response that has been previously extinguished as a function of time (Kimble, 1961). With respect to assertion training, the response we are talking about is anxiety. For example, if a client reports lowered levels of anxiety while successfully role-playing a particular situation, we would predict that some of this anxiety would return by the next session just as a function of the intervening time, assuming that there was no between-session practice to reinforce the gains made. Although we would predict that the anxiety level would not be as high as before, we would still expect the spontaneous recovery of some of this anxiety. By overlearning the situation within a given session and then repeating this rehearsal during subsequent sessions, it is our belief that the anxiety level is not as likely to "recover" to the point where it will interfere with the individual's ability to successfully assert himself in the environment outside of the assertion group at some future time.

Secondly, role rehearsal exercises are not real-life situations, and people are able to discriminate that fact. Even if they are totally desensitized and report no anxiety in the group situation, they will probably experience some anxiety in their outside environment when they encounter that situation. By repeatedly practicing and overlearning the assertive responses to the point where these responses become almost automatic, we hope to increase the probability that these assertive responses will more readily generalize to real-life situations.

Along these lines, we frequently have the client practice goal-related situations that are much more difficult than he is likely to encounter in the outside world. This procedure is carried out in a hierarchical manner whereby we progress, step by step, from easier situations to harder situations, gradually continuing beyond the limits that the client might normally expect to experience. For example, in working with a client who reports difficulty in defending herself against unfair name-calling from her husband, we would set up a hierarchy of situations and people ranging from easy to difficult.

During the initial role-playing situations, the name-calling directed to the client would be minor and would come from the person in the group who elicits the least amount of anxiety for the client. The protagonist would then gradually increase the intensity of the name-calling while the client was being coached. When the client could successfully and appropriately assert herself with low levels of anxiety regardless of what was being said, the next person in her hierarchy would be called upon and the process would be repeated. We might continue this process until *all* the members in the group, with the exception of the client's coach, were taking part in this process *simultaneously*. At this point, it is quite likely that the extent of the name-calling would far exceed the behaviors of the spouse. By using a number of different protagonists, each with a different style and assortment of "favorite" names, it is assumed that the client will be better prepared to handle name-calling from her husband as well as from other individuals she may encounter in her environment at some time in the future. In addition, we believe that this intensive practice will help to reduce the spontaneous recovery of anxiety that might occur as a function of time.

As an example of overlearning skills, one of the authors was recently called into court to be an expert witness on behalf of a client in a heated child custody case. He had never been to court before and had a great deal of anticipatory anxiety as a result of watching too many Perry Mason TV reruns. To put it mildly, he was freaking (i.e., SUDS=80)! Believing that a person should practice what he preaches, he asked for help. Consequently, a behavioral rehearsal of a courtroom scene was set up. He took the role of the assertor (i.e., the expert witness), another trainer who had been in court before took the role of the coach, and other members of the group served in the capacity of prosecuting attorney, defense attorney, and judge. During the rehearsal, the "witness" was challenged more times and in more ways than he cares to remember. He was asked some very difficult questions, and in general, given a rough time. This exercise continued until his anxiety was reduced to a SUDS level of 15. Some spontaneous recovery did occur because when the court day appeared two weeks later, his SUDS was again at 60. However, upon taking the stand, he quickly saw that the situation was not nearly as bad as he had anticipated and that the role rehearsal situation had been worse. His SUDS consequently dropped to 15 where it stayed throughout his testimony.

Humor

In our opinion, the more you can utilize humor in your assertion training, the more effective and enjoyable the training will be. Not only is humor incompatible with anxiety (and, therefore, a valuable counter-conditioning agent), but it also helps to enhance the entire morale of the group. There is no good reason that we can see for making assertion training a grim, formal process. On the contrary, we have found that a sense of humor fits in quite nicely with assertion training. We have also observed that other successful therapists doing assertion training also employ a very active sense of humor in running their groups. We cannot tell you what to say or what to do, for that is a very individualistic matter. However, we would like to encourage you to free yourself of many of those old therapy rules, and allow your sense of humor to emerge.

Feedback equipment

As a final aid in behavioral rehearsal, the use of feedback equipment has been found to be very helpful at various times in assertion training. In our groups, this equipment has generally been in the form of an audio recorder which is played back to the individual after he practices some assertive behavior in order to give feedback on voice intonation, volume, and firmness. However, as Alberti & Emmons (1970), Melnick (1973), and Eisler et al. (1974) have indicated, the use of a videotape may be even more effective and useful. When we have been able to use a videotape unit, we

102

have found it to be an extremely valuable tool for working with clients and as a means for teaching others to do assertion training. Also, as O'Connor (1969) demonstrated with young children and Rathus (1973b) showed with college women, it is possible to train individuals to become more assertive by having them view or listen to others who can successfully assert themselves.

In addition to the audio and video equipment, we have also occasionally used biofeedback equipment when first teaching an individual how to relax or how to maintain a state of relaxation while doing some behavioral rehearsal (we have used a portable heart-rate machine for this purpose). Although this biofeedback equipment has only been used on one person at a time, it does appear to be of value, even in a group situation, when the individual is having difficulty getting in touch with his internal physiological states. We have recently envisioned the possibility of having clients monitor some of their reactions to stress outside of therapy through the use of small, portable units. We have not yet been able to research this idea on a systematic basis; however, some of our initial attempts at this look quite encouraging.

The whole area of feedback and the use of feedback equipment in assertion training is very exciting. We suspect that, within the near future, a considerable amount of research in this area will be forthcoming.

8 Basic nonverbal assertive behaviors

Eye contact

The initial exercise we asked you to visualize in Chapter 2 dealt with eye contact. This was very appropriate since eye contact is one of the most basic and essential assertive behaviors. Unfortunately, many individuals, especially nonassertive individuals, have very poor eye contact. As a result, they are often perceived as being nervous and uncertain of themselves which, in turn, may prompt others to take advantage of them. Another consequence of poor eye contact is that both the individual with poor eye contact and the person with whom he is talking may feel very uncomfortable during a conversation.

Poor eye contact may be due to high levels of anxiety or it may be due to cultural differences where direct eye contact is deemed socially inappropriate in certain circumstances. In most interpersonal situations in our society, good eye contact is an asset rather than a deficit. As such, we have tried to teach this skill to our clients. Fortunately, it is a relatively easy skill to teach (both to hospitalized patients and to others as well).

Let us assume an individual in one of our assertion groups is to practice establishing and maintaining better eye contact. Let us also assume that we have already introduced and discussed the use of SUDS. The first thing we would ask the client to do is pick out someone in the room with whom he believes he would feel relatively comfortable (i.e., low SUDS). We would then ask him to go over to that person, sit down in front of the other individual at a comfortable distance, and keep his eyes on the ground. When this has been accomplished, we would proceed with the following instructions.

With your vision focused on the ground, I would like you to rate your SUDS at this moment. (Pause) OK, take a couple of nice deep breaths, let the air out of your lungs slowly, and again rate your SUDS. (Pause) What I am going to do is teach you how to become more comfortable giving another person direct eye contact. I will do this by having you look at different areas while at the same time trying to keep your anxiety level low. Just listen to my directions, and follow what I ask you to do. If at any time your SUDS gets above 50, just raise your hand so I will know to slow down.

Once again, with your eyes on the ground, rate your SUDS. (Pause) Fine, now look at the other person's ankles. (Pause) Look back down to the ground. (Pause) Now look at the person's ankles again. (Pause) Good. Now look at the person's knees. (Pause) Now look at the person's stomach. (Pause) Now look at the knees. (Pause) Look at the stomach again. (Pause) Rate your SUDS. Look at the person's left shoulder. (At this point, the client is apt to hesitate until he figures out which is the left shoulder. This is intentional in that thinking through a problem is incompatible with anxiety.) SUDS. Look back down at the ground. (Pause) Now look at the right shoulder. (Pause) Now look over the person's head about two feet. (Pause) SUDS. Good.

Now look back at the person's waist. (Pause) Look at the person's chin. (Pause) SUDS. Look at the person's left ear. (Pause) SUDS. Look back down to the ground. (Pause) Look at the person's forehead. (Pause) Look now at the right ear. (Pause) SUDS. Look back at the person's shoulder. (Pause) Now look at the left ear. (Pause) Now the right ear. (Pause) SUDS. Whether you realize it or not, to go from the left ear to the right ear, you had to pass the eyes. Look back at the ground. (Pause) Rate your SUDS. Look at the person's eyes.

(Brief pause) Excellent. Now look back at the ground. (Pause) SUDS. Look at both eyes. (Pause) SUDS. Now look over the person's head about six inches. (Pause) Now back to the eyes. (Pause) SUDS. Look at the person's ear. Now back to the eyes and hold that eye contact. (Pause) Good. Now look back at the chin. (Pause) Now at the forehead. (Pause) Now at the eyes again. (Pause) SUDS. Look back at the ground. (Pause) Rate your SUDS. Look back at the person's eyes and this time give the person a smile. (Pause) SUDS. Now look up here for a moment.

Actually, when you are more than four or five feet away from another person and are looking anywhere within a radius of six inches of the person's eyes, he will be unable to tell whether or not you are giving him direct eye contact. Let me demonstrate. Where am I looking? (At this point the therapist looks at the chin, forehead, or ear of someone across the room—it is very difficult to tell where the gaze is being focused.) Consequently, if you are in a situation where giving direct eye contact begins to make you feel nervous, don't look down at the ground or entirely away from the person. Instead focus your eye contact on the person's chin or forehead until you feel comfortable giving direct eye contact again.

What I want you to do this next week is practice giving better eye contact. Do this with people you know, as well as with strangers you may pass in the street or talk to for a short time. Begin by looking at some part of the body other than their eyes—such as the nose, ear or forehead. If your SUDS is low, then give brief eye contact and try to hold it for awhile. If your SUDS gets high (over 40), then look at the forehead, chin, or ear for awhile before going back to the eye contact. Even when you are able to maintain direct eye contact without feeling tense, it is best to break this eye contact occasionally in order to avoid the other person's feeling uncomfortable due to your staring. Try to practice this as much as possible during the coming week. Keep a record of some of these experiences with your corresponding SUDS, and let's see how things are going next week.

These instructions need not be followed verbatim. The important points to remember are to gradually shape more direct eye contact by progressing in small steps, to constantly monitor the SUDS, to occasionally use distracting stimuli (e.g., "left shoulder"), and to move at a relatively quick pace (such as in the "Simon Says" game which this exercise closely resembles).

Once direct eye contact can be comfortably maintained, teach the individual to look away briefly from time to time without looking down at the ground or off into space and have him occasionally blink his eyes to avoid the image of a doll or Zombie. In most cases, this exercise is introduced during one of the early group sessions (it is a good group training procedure to start with), and it is sometimes repeated one or two more times at a later date (with a hospitalized population, more frequent practice may be required). As indicated in the dialogue, we tend to give some practice in this area as a homework assignment, and, on some occasions, we have had the client practice direct eye contact with people on TV before practicing with "live" people in his environment: The news programs are good for this.

Handshake

Another basic nonverbal assertive behavior that we work on in the early sessions is a firm handshake. Have you ever shaken hands with a limp "dead fish"? Unfortunately, many of us have, and the limp "dead fish" turns out to be someone else's hand. For some individuals, the idea of a firm handshake will immediately result in their anxiety level going up. Perhaps it is the touching or closeness they are trying to avoid, or perhaps it is the fear of getting their hands squeezed too tightly by someone who is trying to evaluate his strength index. For those who fit in the latter category, there is a secret to avoiding unnecessary pain while shaking hands. The secret is simply to place your hand as far into the other person's hand as possible. By doing this, the point of leverage is altered, and it is much more difficult for the other person to exert enough pressure on your hand to really hurt you. Besides, by doing this, you get away from the limp handshake which can be very unnerving (after all shaking hands with a "limp fish" is not very high on the social desirability scale of most individuals).

This of course does not deal with questions such as who offers the hand first when a man and woman meet (our etiquette books and resource people keep giving us different answers on this), how to deal with cultural differences in this area, or what to do if the client has a phobia to touching. We have found, however, that by practicing firm handshakes and good eye contact in the group for a while, many of these other problems can be discussed and resolved. In terms of cultural differences, once these differences have been recognized and discussed, the client is better able to discriminate when and where the different approach behaviors may be appropriate. In terms of the phobia to touching and closeness, it may be necessary to do some systematic relaxation training or systematic desensitization before the individual is able to comfortably reach out and come in physical contact with another person.

Touching

We have found that physical contact is one of the most valuable assertive behaviors to teach other people. It is amazing how many adults report that they received very little affectionate touching and hugging when they were children. As a result, these individuals often feel very uncomfortable in touching others as they grow older, including their own spouses and children. Yet, the touch of another human being can be one of the most positive "warm fuzzies" a person can receive. We try to model and promote touching in our groups whenever possible.

Almost all of the touching we work with is of a non-sexual nature (e.g., touching someone on the arm or shoulder, feeling comfortable in hugging a friend). However, when a client is working on establishing a more intimate

109

relationship, we may also deal with the more intimate aspects of touching, which can be approached in a hierarchical manner as with other assertive behaviors. Clients who are extremely phobic of the opposite sex will often avoid even the slightest touch or brushing of another person's body. Upon any physical contact whatsoever, the individual may flinch or noticeably stiffen. The long-range consequence for this type of reaction will probably be to hinder the relationship.

Therefore, for those individuals in our groups who express an uneasiness in physical contact and would like to change this, we model and systematically practice sitting close to someone, touching, holding hands, hugging, and some simple, publicly appropriate affectionate responses. This desensitization procedure can be carried out ethically and professionally. We are not trying to imply that every interaction should involve physical contact. However, we do feel that touching is one of the most neglected and yet most meaningful ways of interacting with another person. As such, we try to model and promote this behavior throughout our sessions.

One situation in particular where we use touching is when we are coaching someone who is doing behavioral rehearsal. An occasional touch on the shoulder or arm is one of the most effective and supporting feedback cues we can give to that individual. Also, as Ritter (1969) has shown in desensitizing phobias, physical contact can also serve to reduce the client's anxiety level. Interestingly, this touching while coaching has been one of the more difficult behaviors to teach other therapists in our workshops. We hope that if you are comfortable touching others, you will utilize this modality in your assertion training. If, on the other hand, you are not comfortable touching others, we would suggest you make this one of your own personal "homework" assignments.

Body space

Another set of nonverbal behaviors is body space. When an individual begins talking to someone else (e.g., at a party), he will automatically stand at a comfortable distance from that other person. For some individuals, this distance is closer than for others. For example, a nonassertive individual will tend to stand farther away from the other person whereas the aggressive individual may choose to stand intimidatingly close. You can determine where your client's comfort zone is by having him stand up, walk over to someone, and begin talking. While the two individuals are talking, ask each of them to take a step closer to one another and rate their SUDS. Then ask each to take two steps backward and rate their SUDS. Following this procedure, you can get a pretty good idea as to the boundaries of the "comfort zone" for this client with this specific other person, recognizing that the client's comfort zone may vary depending upon the identity of the other person. This distance can be very important when the client is attempting to begin or maintain an interaction with someone. By standing too far away, there is a greater tendency for both individuals to be distracted or for other people to enter into the conversation. By standing too close or off to the side, the other person may begin to feel uncomfortable and, consequently, may try to move away or terminate the interaction.

Have you ever noticed yourself feeling vaguely uncomfortable when you're in the presence of a policeman—even when you are not getting a ticket? One reason for this, perhaps, is that policemen are trained to stand at a safe distance from a person they approach so as to avoid getting hit or stabbed. Sometimes they stand very close so that they can take the person into custody quickly if necessary. When they stand more than an arm's length away, they tend to stand off the person's right shoulder instead of facing the person directly. They do this because most people are right-handed, and if the individual attempts to hit the officer, the officer is in a better position to make the necessary moves in order to handcuff the person. Because they have learned this stance as part of their survival skills and tend to use it repeatedly during their on-duty hours, there is a greater likelihood that, even when they are off work, they will tend to adopt this body space as their comfort zone.

We have not given you this tidbit of information just to make you feel more at ease when talking with a policeman at a party, but rather to illustrate that all of us have developed comfort zones where we feel most safe and protected. When this zone is a mutually comfortable territory, there are no problems. However, when this distance causes some discomfort for one or both individuals, the interaction may suffer as a result. Consequently, in working with this body space, we try to teach the individual to better meet his needs by standing at various distances as well as being perceptive to the comfort zones of others.

Body posture, facial expressions, and voice characteristics

There are almost an infinite number of body postures and facial expressions that a person can assume. Essentially, we try to teach the individual to adopt a body posture and facial expression that correspond with the feeling and message the person is trying to convey: If an individual is trying to be tender, this does not correspond with a rigid, stiff posture; if the person is trying to be firm, this does not correspond with slouched shoulders and poor eye contact; if the person is trying to refuse a request, this does not correspond with a nervous smile. Along these lines, it may be useful at some point for the client to practice conveying his message without using any words, but, instead, using only body movements and gestures. As the nonverbal communication falls into place, the words can then be added.

In working with some of these nonverbal aspects of communication, the use of videotape equipment can be very helpful. If you have some videotape equipment available, we would suggest that you not only observe how your clients interact with one another, but also how you interact with your clients. However, in using the videotape equipment, we would like to offer a word of caution. When individuals first observe themselves on videotape, they are often very uncomfortable with what they see. This is perhaps the first time that they have had the opportunity to see themselves as others see them, and, under these circumstances, they can

112

become painfully aware of many of their nuances and gestures. At such times, there is a tendency to be extremely critical of oneself—more critical than necessary. Consequently, when you use the videotape, try to point out as many positive things you see as possible and do not just dwell on the negative properties. If the interaction you happen to tape is a poor one, don't replay the situation over and over again until the person becomes really depressed and wants to avoid observing himself in the future! Instead, go over the scene once, twice at the most, and then with the pointers you have given, have the person role-play the situation again while using the videotape. After the person has made some definite progress, you may want to replay one of the earlier scenes primarily to show the improvement that has been made. The use of videotape equipment can be very helpful and effective: The individual may change many of his behaviors just by observing himself and without much discussion. But be certain to give a lot of positive feedback, as well as a few suggestions for behaviors to observe and possibly change.

In working with voice characteristics—not *what* is said, but *how* it is said—we deal primarily with volume, tone, and inflection. We have found that many of the individuals in our groups, especially the nonassertive individuals, typically talk in a quiet, timid voice—regardless of whether they are trying to be tender or very angry. Consequently, we try to teach them that different situations and circumstances dictate the use of different voice characteristics. One method of enhancing the use of a louder voice is by having the client practice a situation while a tape recorder is turned on, and then having the client listen to the replay of the interaction. The client can then be encouraged and coached to speak a bit louder during a retake of the situation, and this can be repeated several times until the client is able to reach a situationally appropriate volume level.

As with other skills that are overlearned, the client may be coached to exaggerate the volume level for awhile so that he can test the limits of a louder voice and so that he becomes less frightened of hearing himself speak in such a voice. Two variations of this procedure which we have used at times involve gradually moving the microphone farther away from the client, thus requiring him to speak louder in order to be recorded (note: you need a recorder that *does not* have an automatic volume level for this), and having the client move to an outer room and carry on a conversation with someone in the group through a closed door. We have even gone so far as having the client move two offices away and speak through two closed doors. Interestingly, when we have practiced this latter procedure, we often find that the client becomes much more appropriately animated in his conversation.

The pitch of the words, the amount of quavering in the voice, and the stress on different syllables in the words can also be very important variables. These aspects of communication are practiced in a similar manner to the other non-verbal characteristics through the use of behavioral rehearsal, coaching, shaping, and the employment of feedback equipment. For example, the following excerpt deals with a client who is experiencing some difficulty in modulating her voice level.

Th: Kit, you have just been talking about a situation where your roommate has not been doing a fair share of cleaning the apartment, and you would like to have her spend a little more time on this task each week. You have also indicated that Pat in our group would elicit the least amount of SUDS were you to role-play and practice making a request to do more of the cleaning. What I would like you to try now is practice making such a request, assuming that Pat is your roommate and that the two of you are comfortably talking about some changes each of you would like to see in your living arrangement.

You have done some role-playing before, so you know that as you get into this situation you may begin to feel some of the same discomfort that you would experience in the actual situation. However, as you also know, the purpose of this behavioral rehearsal is to give you repeated practice so that your discomfort, if it occurs at all, will be well within tolerable limits. Remember, if you get stuck or if your SUDS gets too high, I will serve as your coach and come to your aid. Now given that you are about to make your feelings known to Pat, what is your SUDS?

Kit: 10.

Th: That sounds good. Pat, since Kit's SUDS is very low at this point, I would like you to offer some minor resistance to her request. However, when you think you would back off from this resistance in your own environment outside of this office, I want you to do so. Also, if I think you are coming on too strong, I will signal you to back off a bit. At this point, Pat, what is your SUDS and do you want a coach to help you play the roommate role?

Pat: My SUDS is 10, and I do not think I will need a coach to help me out with this one.

Th: Fine. Kit, do you know what you want to say?

Kit· Yes, I want to make a direct statement to Pat that I feel I am doing a disproportionate amount of the housework and that I would like Pat to make more of an effort to help out.

Th: Sounds very good. I am going to turn on the tape recorder so that you can get some feedback after the interaction is over. OK, let's begin.

Kit: Pat, lately I feel that I have been doing most of the housework around here. I would really appreciate it if you would spend some more time each week cleaning the living room and the kitchen area.

Th: Good. What you said was clear and to the point. When you made your statement, your voice level was low so I would like you to raise your volume a little more as you go on. What is your SUDS?

Kit: 20.

Th: OK, that is not too high for you. Take a deep breath while Pat responds to your statement.

Pat: Gee, the house looks all right to me.

Kit: That is because you are a slob!

Th: Stop. Kit, by calling Pat names like that, you begin to infringe upon her dignity, and, besides, name-calling is likely to make the other person defensive and want to fight back. Try saying something like, "Evidently our standards are somewhat different. I really would appreciate it if you would spend a little more time on those two areas of the house when it is your turn to clean." By the way, the fact that you pointed out specific areas of the house that you would like to see improved upon was excellent. OK, try restating your last sentence to Pat.

Kit: Pat, our standards for a clean house are evidently different. I would appreciate it if you would spend more time cleaning the kitchen and living room when it is your week to clean.

Pat: I don't know why we are arguing about this—it just doesn't seem that important.

Kit: It is important to me.

Th: The content of your response that time was super, and your volume was generally louder than before. Very good. What is your SUDS now?

Kit: Not high.

Th: Please give me a specific number.

Kit: 15.

Th: OK, that is certainly within a tolerable range for you. When you said, "It is important to me," you let Pat know exactly how you were feeling which is great. However, you almost whispered the word "me." I would like to replay the recording at this point so that you can hear the interaction between the two of you. Then we will start again where Pat says, "It doesn't seem that important." I would like you to say the same super thing you said before, but try to speak even a bit louder than before and this time emphasize the word "me" more.

In this area of training as with other areas, it is important to move in small steps and to constantly monitor the person's SUDS. Also, the trainer must be ready to come to the person's aid if he becomes very anxious, says something inappropriate, or is at a loss for words.

Timing

A person may have the correct words, body posture, and gestures and still come across inappropriately if the *timing* of the assertive response is incorrect. Just as the individual must learn *what* to do, he must also learn *when* to do it. This is, perhaps, a more difficult skill to teach, but, yet, it is a very important factor. For example, asking the boss for a raise right after he knowingly had a fight with another employee may prove to be disastrous. Likewise, a wife who wishes to inform her husband that she wants him to do more of an equal share of work around the house can probably pick a better time than when he first walks in the door. Consequently when working on assertive skills, especially when the client has a specific situation in mind, it is very important to discuss when and under what circumstances the assertive action is more likely to produce favorable results rather than punitive consequences. For even if the assertion components are in order, they are of only limited value if the timing is not also correct.

Timing can be practiced in a number of situations: when to enter a three-way conversation, interrupting a situation to give a message, changing the subject of a conversation, and so forth. Through discussion and the practice of situations such as this within the group, the individual will, hopefully, acquire a better sense of timing in his ongoing activities outside of the group.

9 Conversation skills
and other relationship skills

Sequence of practice

The manner in which we present specific assertive procedures varies from time to time; however, one sequence has generally appeared to be very effective for us (this sequence can be used for individual as well as group assertion training). Given that we have a specific skill in mind which we believe is appropriate to the problem area described by the client (e.g., "I have trouble meeting and talking with people, especially at a party or other social situation"), we begin by setting up the situation and asking the client to *visualize* how he would typically respond (the client is also asked to rate his SUDS as he visualizes the scene). This first part of the sequence corresponds to the visualization exercises we asked you to do in the second chapter of this book. The next step is to describe some of the basic components of the skill we want to work on (e.g., asking open-ended questions), and this is followed by a demonstration whereby the trainers model an assertive procedure for the group members to observe. After the demonstration has been carried out and briefly discussed, the client is once again asked to visualize the same situation, keeping track of his SUDS and trying to utilize as many of the modeled components as possible. When this has been completed, the client then role-plays the procedure while being coached. It is very important that this behavioral rehearsal be *actively* coached and carried out in such a way that the client receives frequent support and feedback. It is also important that the behavioral rehearsal is carried out in such a manner that the situation itself and the other actors in the role-playing situation do not create high levels of anxiety for the client.

After the client has been coached through this demonstration, the group is often divided into triads with one individual taking the role of the *assertor*, one person acting as a *coach*, and the third person assuming the *recipient* (or *protagonist*) role. The participants then role-play the situation until each person has had the opportunity to be the assertor, the coach, and the recipient. During this time the therapists circulate around the room assisting in the triads when appropriate. This latter step allows for a great deal of group interaction and practice to occur simultaneously, and in addition to the coaching role, it allows individuals to be on the "receiving" as well as on the "giving" end of the assertive responses. This can be very helpful in that individuals are often more willing to respond assertively after they have experienced how it feels to be the recipient of an assertive interaction. This role-playing may be repeated several times if necessary until individuals are able to respond assertively and maintain a low SUDS. However, triad practice should only be used after most, if not all, of the group members can assume the roles of coach and recipient with a certain degree of proficiency and with tolerable levels of anxiety. As a final step, the group practice is discussed, and an attempt is made to correct or respond to any problems or difficulties which may have occurred.

The preceding sequence is not used every time a new procedure is introduced; however, we have utilized it quite frequently, and we have found it to be very effective in introducing some of the various procedures we wish to present for our clients to observe and experience.

Conversational skills

There are a number of component behaviors to establishing, maintaining, and terminating conversations. There are also a number of additional skills which can serve to enhance a new or well-established relationship between two or more individuals. In reality, these different behaviors can overlap and intertwine with one another during the course of any interaction. However, for training and writing purposes, we have separated these components into *conversation skills* and *additional relationship skills*.

An individual possessing conversational skills is often regarded as being "sociable," "fun," "friendly," and, in some cases, even "charismatic." As a result, this individual is more likely to have a greater number of acquaintances and friends than a person lacking in the ability to initiate and sustain conversations. In most cases, before you are able to make a friend, you must first talk to the person and get to know him. Conversely, the "stranger" must learn something about you.

Many individuals who have been in our assertion groups report the feeling that they have no effect in a dialogue. They describe themselves as being "leaves in the wind," blown about at the mercy of the stranger with whom they are attempting to talk. If the stranger is easy to talk to, they may be able to keep a conversation going. However, if the stranger is not eager or skillful in talking with them, they walk away feeling anxious and frustrated. Other individuals in our groups report that they are able to meet new people only under certain ritualistic circumstances, such as being introduced by a mutual friend two or three consecutive times, being in a personally comfortable setting, talking about certain noncontroversial subjects, or after taking four drinks. Certainly these latter individuals are better off than having no way of meeting other people, but the probability of their requirements occurring on a regular basis is rather slim. These individuals, too, feel the lack of personal power to change the course of a dull or anxious encounter into an enjoyable meeting and conversation.

We feel that being able to comfortably talk with others is a skill that can be extremely important for those individuals who have relegated themselves to the roles of social wallflowers and isolates. With the proper skills and moderately low anxiety, such people can increase the probability of initiating friendships and enhancing relationships in a variety of social situations. These skills are applicable whenever people meet people. Consider the number of times you encounter a stranger in the course of a day. Whether it is a man meets woman scenario, student meets professor, or an interaction involving a grocery clerk, landlord, policeman, doctor, or lawyer, the ability to talk to people in order to express what you are feeling and thinking can potentially increase your pleasure and welfare in life.

Before we describe some behaviorally defined components of an interaction, there is an important point to consider. Although some of the following skills will increase the probability of starting and maintaining a conversation with someone, they will not insure an extended dialogue or guarantee a resulting friendship. If the person you are attempting to talk with does not want to participate, a conversation will probably not occur. Similarly if the "stranger" and you cannot find some mutual interests, a friendship will probably not develop. Therefore, a risk is taken by a person attempting to form a relationship with someone else. This risk is one of rejection or the possible fear of rejection. Of course, the risk of being alone and isolated is also present if no socialization attempts are made. This risk must be attended to by all assertion trainers working with clients who are developing interaction skills. Therefore, developing reasonable and manageable homework assignments designed to maximize the chances for success in this area is of utmost importance.

In working with individuals who show a deficit in being able to establish and maintain enjoyable conversations, we typically break down the process of a conversation into the following observable components which we have labeled conversation skills.

Skill one: Open-ended questions

In order to find out information about another individual, asking questions is often necessary. However, there are at least two different kinds of questions you can ask—the *open-ended* question and the *close-ended* question. A close-ended question is one that can be answered with a simple one-word answer or grunt: "Do you come to the beach here often?" "Do you like that book?" "Is this the first time you have been to one of Melvin's parties?" "Do you like the weather when it is windy like this?" Close-ended questions such as these often elicit a "Yes," "No," or "Uh-huh" response. As a result, if the individual does not elaborate on his "Yes," "No," or "Uh-huh" response, you will acquire only a minimal amount of information about him. Also, if close-ended questions are asked one after another, the recipient of these questions may begin to feel as if he were being interrogated. Consequently, he may begin to back off from the interaction. One or two of these close-ended questions may be appropriate at the beginning of a conversation in order to get the conversation started. However, if a number of questions are going to be asked, we recommend the use of an open-ended question whenever possible.

An open-ended question is one that cannot easily be answered by a monosyllabic reply: "What is it about this beach that you enjoy?" or "How do you feel about the movement for equal rights to women in our society?" If you received a "Yes" or "No" reply from these questions, you would probably think that the person was a bit odd (or did not want to talk with you in the first place). Open-ended questions are usually much more difficult to answer with a simple, short reply; consequently, you are more likely to gain additional information about the individual when asking these open-ended questions. Actually, there are two categories of open-ended questions. The first category includes those questions that begin with the words or ideas of *who, what, when,* or *where:* "Who do you recommend I go to in order to get my car fixed?" "What is it about sailing that is so exciting?" "When and where is the fishing best around here?" "Where Is the bathroom?" The second type of open-ended question begins with *how* or *why,* such as "How did you get into that business in the first place?" or "Why do you think I am mad at you?" *How* and *why* questions tend to elicit detailed explanations from the individual; consequently they give the individual an opportunity to tell you a great deal about himself. As such, they can be the most useful type of questions in leading to a comfortable interaction between two or more individuals.

Skill two: Attending to free information

Free information is information given by another individual which goes beyond the question being asked or is given without being solicited. If, for example, you asked, "How do you like this windy weather we have been having?" and the other person replied by saying, "I'd like it a lot better if I was out sailing on my boat rather than painting my house this weekend," you have obtained four bits of free information. The person likes to sail and has a sailboat, he owns a house, and is presently painting his house. The free information that is given to you can be on a superficial level: "I don't like to paint." It can also be of a more personal nature: "Since my recent divorce, doing housework has really become depressing." After receiving some free information from an individual, you are at a choice point. You can either continue talking about the topic you were on, or you can begin talking about the free information. For example, with the question asked on the weather, you could continue talking about the weather, or you could branch the conversation onto the topic of sailing, owning a home, or doing housework. Where you go with the information depends upon your personal interests and your interests in knowing more about the other person.

The ability to listen for and respond to selected pieces of free information is an important factor in starting and maintaining enjoyable conversations. People do not normally volunteer information they do not wish to talk about. Consequently, if we receive some information from the other individual freely, it is usually a sign that it is all right to discuss that topic. At times we may avoid discussing information given by the other individual which we consider to be embarrassing or of a too personal nature. If the information is too embarrassing or personal for your comfort, that is one thing. However, if the other person freely volunteered the information, it is unlikely that it is too embarrassing or personal for him.

For example, once while we were demonstrating conversation skills in front of a large group using a volunteer from the audience, a question was asked regarding the volunteer's interests. In answering the question, the individual commented that she had been recently divorced and had two small children at home. The workshop leader purposely avoided any conversation about her divorce and, instead, began talking about the children. In discussing the demonstration afterwards, the workshop leader stated that he had avoided the topic of divorce because he felt it would have been uncomfortable for the participant to talk about this in front of the larger group. However, the participant in the demonstration stated that she would not have been uncomfortable at all with the subject and, in fact, she felt free to talk about it. Although it was well within the leader's rights to avoid the divorce topic, and in this situation it did not seem to hamper the conversation, he forgot that free information is usually given willingly and, as such, it can be taken as an invitation to pursue that topic.

This does not mean that all free information needs to be discussed. In fact, some individuals may repeatedly volunteer free information that you do not want to touch with a ten-foot pole: "Do you want to hear about my fifth sexual conquest of the week?" On the other hand, one of the basic skills in good conversations is at least listening for the free information given by the other person. If the information is interesting, then talk about it or store it in the back of your mind so that you can come back to it later. If the free information is not of interest to you, then skip it and listen for some additional free information which is more interesting to you. It is well to remember that if you pursue a topic in which you are totally uninterested or with which you feel extremely uncomfortable, there is a greater likelihood of a dead-end conversation, boredom, or high anxiety.

Skill three: Giving self-disclosure
Self-disclosure is free information that you give *about yourself* during the course of a conversation. Consider the following interaction between Milford (M) and Wetley (W). As the reader, put yourself in Wetley's position, and see how you feel about Milford.

Scene: Waiting for a bus somewhere in Los Angeles

M: Hi, are you waiting for the bus to San Diego?

W: Yes, why?

M: I was just wondering if you knew if the bus usually runs on time.

W: Well, I travel on this bus at least once or twice a week, and it is usually late. (Free information as to how often he uses that bus.) I sure hope it's on time today because I have an important business appointment in San Diego at 3:00 p.m. (More free information.)

M: (Responding to some of the free information) What business are you in that makes you travel to San Diego so often?

W: I'm a traveling horseshoe salesman for Sears. (Free information as to what he does and for whom he works.)

M: Huh! What exactly do you do?

W: Well, I sell primarily to large farms and to distributors in my region. I travel a lot since there aren't many horses around here. (Free information.)

M: Do you like it?

W: It's a living. I don't like leaving my family so much, and I hate horses. (Two more pieces of free information.)

M: (Deciding to stay with the topic of horseshoes rather than following up on Wetley's family or dislike of horses) Say, how is the recession affecting the sales of horseshoes?

The conversation could continue like this until the bus arrived. How did you feel about Milford by the end? Milford has managed to start a conversation, ask several open-ended questions, and is following his free information leads well. However, one knows very little about Milford because he did not share any free information about himself which would have given the "shoe salesman" an opportunity to know him better. Actually, all you really know about Milford is that he is talking to Wetley and is probably on his way to San Diego.

If, on the other hand, Milford had given some self-disclosure, then the conversation may have been quite different. Both parties could have learned about each other and shared in the mutual exchange of information and feelings.

M: How is the recession affecting the horseshoe business?

W: It doesn't affect it very much at all. Horses always need shoes, and sales are actually up since people are buying more horses lately. Actually, I am making more money now than I have for the past four years. (Free information.)

M: No kidding. (Here comes Milford's self-disclosure.) Maybe I should change professions. I'm a psychologist, and our business is way down lately.

W: Gee, I have a cousin back East who is a psychologist, and I just assumed that his business would increase at times like this. (Free information.)

M: Well maybe things back East are different, but all I know is that, as a psychologist in a private practice, my business is way off. (Free information.)

W: What are you going to do about it?

M: Write a book about how to start conversations with strangers.

The second half of the conversation included some free information from both parties and was, in our opinion, a more equitable and enjoyable interchange.

In order to get more information from the other person, you must be willing and able to give some information about yourself. To what degree the conversation stays on a superficial level or moves to a more personal level depends upon the type of information that is mutually shared. Typically, conversations between individuals who do not know one another very well will move from a superficial to a more personal level, assuming that both individuals contribute increasingly greater amounts of personal information. We suggest that the information disclosed be gradually increased in intimacy if you are trying to move from a superficial relationship to a more intimate relationship. On each new level of intimacy disclosed, it is wise to pause and take the other individual's response into account. If he is receptive and responds similarly, then you may want to disclose more intimate information. It is unlikely that a comfortable conversation will last very long if one individual is relating personal information—"My marriage sure is rotten"—and the other individual is responding on a superficial level—"Yeah, I have an automobile that is rotten." In such situations, one of the individuals needs to adjust his level of communication or the interaction will usually terminate. Likewise, if one individual comes on with some very personal information or questions at the very beginning of a conversation, the other individual may not be prepared for this, and may, consequently, try to back away from the interaction, as in the following scene between Otis (O) and Zola (Z).

Scene: After the first day of class at a local university

O: Hi, my name is Otis. All during the class I was sitting across the room noticing how attractive you looked. (Self-disclosure and compliment.) Since this is the first day of class and because I feel uncomfortable until I get to know a few people, I wanted to come over and introduce myself. (Self-disclosure.)

Z: Thank you very much for the compliment, Otis. I know very few people in this room too. My name is Zola. (Self-disclosure.)

O: Say, Zola. My apartment is just around the block from the university. How about coming over to my place tonight? We can smoke some pot and listen to records while we try out my new water bed. (Self-disclosure, free information.)

Z: Thanks for the invitation—but no thanks. I want to go to the library now. Goodbye.

In the above interaction, it is possible that Zola was attracted to Otis and would have liked to know him better. However, by Otis coming on so strong and so quickly, this particular relationship may never have the opportunity to develop. Therefore, in giving and receiving self-disclosures and asking questions, it is important to balance what is said with what is received. As a rule of thumb in giving self-disclosures, we suggest that a person give about as much free information as he receives in a conversation. If too little free information is given, the other individual will begin to feel as if he were being interrogated. On the other hand, if too much free information is provided without giving the other individual the opportunity to respond, the conversation may become too one-sided.

Skill four: Changing topics

Individuals will often terminate a conversation prematurely when they run out of questions to ask or when the conversation begins to focus on an area in which they are not interested. Most initial conversations, especially those between two strangers, take awhile to get started. Consequently, before a common topic of interest is found, there may be several silences and several periods where topics are briefly picked up and then dropped. Just knowing that this is a common occurrence helps to alleviate much of this problem. It is also important to teach people that they have some control over the direction the conversation takes, especially if only two people are involved in the conversation. If they are not satisfied with the current topic of conversation, asking another open-ended question, following up on some free information that has been stored away, making a self-disclosure statement regarding another topic, or simply stating, "I am really interested in hearing more about. . . ." will often serve to move the topic of conversation to another area which is more satisfying or interesting for the individual, as in the following interaction between Joan (J) and Bill (B).

Scene: An informal house party

J: Hi, Bill. What have you been doing lately?

B: Well, during the summer I do a lot of ocean fishing. Just last week I went ocean fishing about 100 miles south of here. Unfortunately, I was sick during the first half of

129

the trip and I didn't catch any fish; however, after I was feeling better, I had a nice time.

Note: In this last sentence, Bill has given three bits of free information about his trip.

J: I went ocean fishing once when I was younger, but I really did not enjoy it what with the rough water and the smell of engine fumes. What do you find enjoyable about fishing—especially since you were sick and didn't catch any fish?

B: Well, I don't normally get sick, and very often I do catch some fish. However, more than anything, it gives me a chance to relax and get away from work.

J: I can certainly understand your desire to get away and relax, although it is hard for me to think of ocean fishing as a way to do this. I would much rather backpack into the mountains where it is quiet and peaceful.

B: Gee, I didn't know that you were into backpacking. That is one of my avid interests too. Where have you done some backpacking?

Note: At this point, Joan has been able to direct the conversation away from ocean fishing which, for her, was not very appealing as a topic of mutual interest.

Skill five: Breaking into ongoing conversations
Another difficulty that is frequently reported involves becoming a part of an ongoing conversation. If the other individuals are open to having another person join in, their body posture and eye contact will often convey this: They will look your way, give you eye contact, and they may realign their bodies so that they are facing you. If this seems to be the case, then it is a matter of being able to stand by, listen to the context of the conversation, and then join in with some appropriate statement of self-disclosure, opinion, interest, or free information when appropriate.

130

Scene: Joan and Bill still talking together at the informal house party

J: Most of my backpacking has been in the Yosemite area; however, I have also done some hiking through Colorado and Oregon.

B: I haven't been to Colorado; however, I was born in Oregon, and I did a lot of backpacking there when I was younger.

Jim: (Who has walked up to this conversation and has stood listening for awhile waiting for an opening to enter the conversation) I didn't know you were from Oregon. I spent one whole summer there a few years ago doing some graduate work. Boy, that part of the country sure is great if you like the out-of-doors. When I was there, I think I spent more time in the woods than I did in the classroom.

In group we often practice this skill by having one client serve as the coach while two people practice their conversation skills. We then ask the coach to join in and become an actual member of the ongoing conversation. After this process has gone on for several moments, we have the individuals form new groups, change roles, and start the whole process over from the beginning. At a later time, in order to approximate the "real world" more, we may have the third person walk up to a conversation that has been going on for a few moments. Even though the third person did not hear the start of the conversation, he tries to become a participating member of this small group. In observing these transitions, we pay close attention to how the individual introduces himself, what information is picked up on, what self-disclosures are made, the timing of the information, and what nonverbal cues are given.

Skill six: Silences (the pregnant pause phobia)
Have you ever become aware of the periods of silence that occur in the course of a conversation? These periods do occur and are quite normal. Sometimes this silence can be uncomfortable, and, at other times, it can feel quite natural.

131

Some individuals, especially those who are inexperienced in conversational skills, are phobic of pauses or silences in a conversation. These individuals feel that they should fill every moment of the conversation with words. They irrationally see silence as a "pregnant pause" that will give birth to personal disaster if they cannot end it immediately. However, almost all conversations, especially those between individuals who are getting to know one another better, have periods of silence. Consequently, giving the individual some relaxation skills and some other things to think about during these silent periods can be extremely useful.

Skill seven: Telling stories

As the individual becomes more comfortable in talking with others, he will begin to talk in longer sentences and may relate some stories, experiences, or jokes. However, in relating these, it is important that each have a *beginning,* a *middle,* and especially an *end.* Some potentially very good stories seem to go on forever. Other stories seem to start from nowhere. Consequently, in relating a personal experience or in telling a story or joke, we encourage the individual to identify in some way a beginning and an end to what he is talking about: "That reminds me of the time I was in Chicago and. . . ." ". . . and that is how I feel about the situation now."

Skill eight: Nonverbal cues

In addition to the verbal content skills, it is important to practice nonverbal conversation skills as well. For example, maintaining appropriate eye contact during the conversation rather than looking out the window or just staring at the other person is important. Other variables such as body space and posture, smiling and head-nodding, animation, voice characteristics, and so forth are also important additions to a smooth-flowing conversation. As such, each of these variables may be worked on separately or as a part of the total procedure in developing more interesting and effective interactions.

Skill nine: Terminating conversations

Simultaneous to teaching the individual how to start a conversation, we also train the individual how to terminate a conversation. Can you recall situations where you felt "cornered" by someone talking to you, and you used some excuse such as "I have to go to the bathroom" or "Oh, I forgot to make a phone call" in order to stop the interaction? Many clients do report situations such as this, and, as a result, they are anxious about entering any conversation where they may later feel trapped or imposed upon. Consequently, before we send them into the "real world," we give them some practice with things to say and do in order to terminate a conversation comfortably. Things to say may involve some "canned" types of verbal responses which may be given at the end of a conversation: "I really have enjoyed talking with you" or "I see someone here whom I have not spoken with for a long time; I would like to continue our conversation later if you are free then." Other solutions may involve a change in the verbal content—less self-disclosure and fewer open-ended questions—as well as some nonverbal cues such as a decrease in eye contact and head-nodding or an increase in body distance from the other person.

It often requires a considerable amount of practice before conversational skills can be carried out successfully. It is also necessary for individuals to experience low levels of anxiety during conversations so that they can hear, process, and respond to the information given. For these reasons, the first attempts at starting and maintaining conversations are confined to role-playing situations within the assertion group. The group serves as a safe haven for this practice since social failure experiences are minimized.

Coaching and *in vivo* desensitization are employed extensively throughout this training period. Initial attempts are structured so that only one skill is required of the client at a time. This enables the trainer to provide initial positive reinforcement for effort as well as some early success. That is, the only task in the mock conversation may be to ask open-ended questions. As the client becomes more skillful in open-ended questions, he may then be asked to listen for and identify free information. When the client can handle this, he would then practice acknowledging and responding to the free information. Later on, the client is asked to carry out the conversation procedures on his own. Only after the client is able to carry out conversations with minimal coaching and low anxiety within the group would he be asked to begin practicing and employing these skills regularly with friends, associates, and with strangers.

One of the early between-session assignments that we frequently give is to go to a public place (e.g., a restaurant, airport, ballgame, laundromat) and listen in on the conversations of others. The task is not to enter into these conversations. Rather, the individual is instructed to listen for any and all free information that is given between the parties. In addition, the client is instructed to think of open-ended questions and self-disclosures that could be given *if* he were actually a part of that conversation.

A more advanced homework assignment would be to ask some open-ended questions or begin a conversation in a situation that is time-limited (e.g., on an elevator, waiting in line in a grocery store, in the service station while you are getting gas). Gradually, the situations can be structured so that the individual is engaging in longer conversations where the potential for more involved or intimate relationships is enhanced, for instance, at a party, talking with someone at work or at a vacation resort. As with most of the behaviors in assertion training, the level and pace of these homework assignments depends upon the individual's anxiety level and existing skills.

Additional relationship skills

Skill ten: Self-praise
It is extremely important that the individual be able to recognize his strengths, interests, and opinions. Remember the exercise where we asked you to visualize describing four positive qualities about yourself to someone else? Were you able to do this without experiencing high levels of anxiety? If not, you may experience some difficulty in talking and sharing with others. Far too often, people are able to recognize and share their weaknesses and shortcomings rather

than their strengths and interests. We try to reverse this process in assertion training. That is, during our conversation practice within and outside of the group, we encourage individuals to share information about their hobbies, interests, strengths, and opinions.

With a little bit of maneuvering, a person should be able to work almost any topic of enjoyable personal interest into a conversation. For example, a few years ago one of the authors spent ten days going down the Colorado River in a rubber raft. Upon returning home, he was so excited about this trip that he worked it into almost every new conversation he entered: "Sherwin, how about going out to lunch?" "Sounds great, I need to gain some of the weight back I lost on my Colorado River expedition."

If individuals come into the group stating they do not have any interests, strengths, hobbies, or opinions, then we try to encourage and give homework assignments that will help them to develop these attributes. For instance, we ask them to read and talk about an article in a magazine that interests them, have them go through and answer Jourard's (1971) Self-Disclosure Questionnaire, or ask them to go to a museum, play, or sports event and relate their experiences. This process is necessary so that the individual can become a better friend to himself and so that he can then have some positive information to share with others. After all, if a person cannot see himself in a positive light, why should he assume that others will see him this way?

Positive free information and self-disclosure can be given in a variety of ways. In our previous examples, much of the free information and self-disclosure came as the result of being asked a question. However, this information can also be given in the process of asking others questions. For example, instead of just saying, "Is this the first time you have been to one of Marvin's parties?" you could say, "I have been to several of Marvin's parties and have never seen you before. Is this the first time you have been here?" Or instead of "Where do you recommend I go to have my car fixed?" you could say, "I have this Porsche which I really enjoy, but it is always in need of a tune-up. Do you know of someone who does good tune-up work on sports cars?" In both of these examples, there is an extra bit of free information which the other person may choose to follow up on then or at some time in the future.

In supporting statements of positive self-disclosure and praise, we are not attempting to reinforce individuals who talk only about themselves and pay no attention to the needs, interests, and positive qualities of others. However, we are deliberately trying to reinforce our clients to recognize that they do possess and can acquire some satisfying and self-fulfilling life experiences. We also encourage them to share these experiences, beliefs, and feelings with others as an alternative to remaining anxious and socially isolated.

Skill eleven: Giving and receiving compliments

At this time, we would like to introduce Jack and Jill. Jill, by the way, is a compliment phobic individual.

Jack: I really like your blouse, Jill.

Jill: This old thing!

Jack: I also like your hair done like that.

Jill: I like your hair, too.

Jack: In addition to the way you look, I really like you, Jill.

Jill: Let's get to work; we have a lot to do.

Jack: Yes, it was really nice of you to help me carry that bucket of water, Jill.

Jill: Anyone could have helped you do that.

Jack: But only you would have pushed me down the hill afterwards, you compliment phobic!

How often have you experienced giving someone a compliment only to have it discarded with an "Oh, that old thing" or "It is really nothing special"? Did you ever feel that you had poor taste after presenting a genuine compliment only to have it thrown back at you with a "You must be kidding" or "You can't really mean that"? Under these kinds of circumstances, you would probably be less likely to compliment that individual in the future. A compliment phobic individual is one who experiences a high rise in his anxiety level when giving or receiving a compliment. As a result of this increased SUDS, the individual will often negate the compliment ("This old thing!"), will respond immediately with a compliment to the other individual ("I like your hair too"), or will just ignore the entire situation ("Let's get to work; we have a lot to do"). Sometimes these responses are carried out in the name of humility: Unfortunately, some individuals are taught that it is improper to be anything except overly humble. At other times, these responses are the result of past experiences where something negative has followed a positive statement. Consider the following situations, which may unfortunately turn an individual off to compliments in the future:

Boss to employee: Hi, Jack. I want you to know that you have been doing an excellent job around here. Your work has been very valuable to us. It really is too bad that business has been off lately, because now we are going to be forced to fire you!

Jack to Jill: Hi, Jill. You really look nice today. Would you lend me $50?

It is no wonder that a person who is frequently subjected to this type of interaction would become cautious of compliments. However, in that this is not the usual course of events, we believe that individuals should be able to give honest compliments to others, as well as acknowledge, accept, and enjoy an honest compliment given to them. It is a sad statement to make about our culture, but oftentimes we feel people are telling the truth when they are criticizing us and think they are not serious when they are giving us compliments. To throw away a compliment is to throw away some of the potential for good feelings. The ability to give a compliment *to others* and the ability to receive a compliment *from others* is a very important social skill. When you compliment someone on his behavior towards you, you are, in a sense, asking him to continue to do that behavior. You are letting him know what you like. If you are important to

137

that other person, the chances of his continuing to behave in that manner are increased. Likewise, when you accept an honest compliment from another, you are listening to important feedback. A compliment, if accepted rather than rejected, can make both the giver and the receiver feel good. It is a mutually rewarding activity. In doing assertion training, we have been very impressed by the changes that occur once an individual is able to receive compliments from and give compliments to others. Frequently, the individual reports feeling happier and being more at ease in social settings. Behaviorally, we will find the individual making more self-complimentary statements in the group as well as completing an increased number of homework assignments outside of the group where he has an opportunity to give and receive these "warm fuzzies."

The first step in aiding a compliment phobic individual is to desensitize the high anxiety level (SUDS) experienced while being complimented. This can be accomplished following a traditional desensitization procedure (Wolpe, 1969) or it can be carried out in an *in vivo* desensitization manner (Wolpe, 1969) during the group session. When receiving a compliment, we ask our clients to maintain eye contact with the other individual, smile, and say "Thank you" or give some other appropriate response following the compliment.

Jack: Jill, I really like the dress you are wearing.

Jill: Thank you, Jack. I just bought it last week when I was on vacation. (Notice the free information.)

We believe this is far more appropriate than negating the compliment ("Oh, you mean this old thing?") or just returning with another compliment:

Jack: Jill, I really like the dress you are wearing.

Jill: Jack, I really like your buckle shoes.

Jack: I like your hair.

Jill: And I like your hair too.

Editor: Enough of this. Go to your room, Jack and Jill.

138

The verbal skill in receiving a compliment is relatively easy to train; the more difficult aspect is lowering the individual's anxiety. Initially, we ask the individual to rank order the other members in the group in terms of the individual from whom he would feel most comfortable in receiving some compliments. Following the client's hierarchy, we then ask the group member who elicits the least amount of anxiety to begin complimenting the phobic individual. When the client is able to maintain a low SUDS level and respond with a comfortable and convincing "Thank you," the next person on the hierarchy is asked to begin complimenting the client. This procedure is followed until the client is able to report a lowered anxiety level to all the *honest* compliments that are bestowed upon him.

In addition to receiving compliments, our clients are also taught how to give compliments to others. In doing this, it is important that the compliments given be honest. If the compliment is not truly honest, then it is best not to give it. Unfortunately, as parents, teachers, spouses, or bosses, we spend a great deal of time trying to "catch" people when they are in error rather than reward them when they are doing something that pleases us. Once this trend is reversed, and the individual begins to "catch" others when they are doing something that pleases him, it is not usually difficult to find several things which merit the positive feedback of a compliment.

Skill twelve: "Strength Bombardment"

Closely related to giving and receiving compliments is the procedure of "Strength Bombardment," developed by Herbert Otto (1969) and described in Alberti & Emmons' (1974) book, *Your Perfect Right*. Essentially, this procedure involves having the client speak about himself in *only* positive terms for a period of one or two minutes while the rest of the group members listen. When the client is finished, the other group members then proceed to describe the positive characteristics they see or like about the individual for one to four minutes. This is done until each person is given the opportunity to experience the "Strength Bombardment."

However, as Alberti & Emmons (1974) have cautioned, the therapist may initially need to do some prompting with the client in order for him to get started, and the trainer should also be prepared to fill in any periods of silence during the group response time: Otherwise the client may actually begin to feel worse.

We have used this procedure in order to strengthen the person's ability to describe some of his positive qualities and to promote a higher level of self-esteem. It is used only after the group members have had the opportunity to interact and get to know one another fairly well so that their responses can, in fact, be genuine. As such, we have found the procedure especially useful prior to a member's "graduation" from the group or as one of the concluding exercises in a workshop. When there has not been sufficient time for each member to receive the feedback from the entire group, we have asked the group members to break into smaller groups (three to five people) with people they have come to know and to carry out this procedure. As another variation of the verbal Strength Bombardment, the individual describes himself in positive terms and then the other group members gather around the individual and express their positive feelings through touch or hugging without the use of any words. As with the other procedures described in this book, one of us brave authors initially demonstrates the self-disclosure and receiving feedback from the group. Although we can justify this on the basis of good modeling, the fact is that this has proven to be one of the nicest "warm fuzzies" we have devised for ourselves in doing these groups; after all, therapists need "warm fuzzies" too.

Skill thirteen: Communication of feelings
with the use of "I" statements

Throughout our work with others, we encourage the verbal expression of open, honest feelings. For the most part, we believe this can be done without the client experiencing negative consequences and without violating the rights and dignity of the other person even when the client is feeling angry, hurt, or disappointed. In setting up a behavioral rehearsal situation, we typically ask the client, "What would you like to say or tell this other person?" Some typical responses to this question are, "I want to tell him that I would like for us to go out more often," or "I want to tell him that I do not like his nagging me about spending so much money," or "I want to be able to tell her how deeply I feel for her." When these individuals are asked to role-play the situation and communicate these feelings, the responses they give are often, "You do not take me out enough," or "Stop your nagging," or "Do you really love me?" These statements tend to make the other person defensive, and they interfere with more open, honest communication.

As part of our assertion training procedures, we encourage using "I" statements, rather than using "You" statements. "I" statements relate specifically to what the person is feeling, thinking, and experiencing. The "I" statements are often avoided because individuals report that they feel more vulnerable after making one of these statements. It is true that an individual is more vulnerable after using the word "I"; however, the use of "I" statements provides a means of communication whereby individuals can become much closer in their relationship rather than further apart. Consider the following interaction between Ruth (R) and Vern (V).

R: You are not taking me out enough.

V: I have been very busy lately.

R: You are always too busy for me lately.

V: You don't seem to appreciate the strain I have been under lately.

R: You are always giving me excuses.

V: You are not so perfect either. How about the fact that you have not cleaned the house in over two weeks?

R: Why don't you help out with the housework if you are so disappointed?

At this point, the interaction between Ruth and Vern is likely to accelerate into an argument of accusations and name-calling. "You" statements tend to promote defensiveness and anger. As such, they are not very conducive to a closer relationship where two individuals are trying to express their feelings and, possibly, their annoyances. Now consider Ruth's complaint, but this time with the exchange of "I" for "You" statements.

R: I am feeling left out by the fact that we do not spend very much time together lately.

V: I have been very busy lately.

R: I can understand that, but I still am feeling left out and hurt by the lack of attention.

V: You don't seem to appreciate the strain I have been under lately.

R: I try to, but it is hard for me when some of my needs for attention are not being met. I think I could be more appreciative of your stress if I felt that we were working on things together.

V: That sounds reasonable. I'll try to include more of your needs as well as my own in the future.

R: I would really appreciate that, and, in turn, I will try to take into account your stress at work. Maybe I can do something to get out of the house more often on my own so that I do not feel so cooped up with the kids.

V: Sounds good. How about enrolling in that music class you were interested in at the college? If you get started with that, maybe we can buy some season tickets for the opera or something like that next fall.

Granted, all conversations do not have such reasonable endings. However, the point is that both Ruth and Vern were able to express some of their needs and irritations without getting into a heated argument.

"I" statements certainly do not solve all the problems of poor communication. However, more and more we are finding that these "I" statements help to facilitate a more open, honest, and mutually satisfying relationship.

142

Skill fourteen: Statements instead of questions

Closely related to the more frequent use of "I" statements, we encourage clients to make statements of their feelings rather than disguising them behind a dishonest question. A dishonest question is one in which we are not willing to equally accept a "Yes" or "No" answer (Knox, 1971) or is a question we ask when we should really be making a statement of self-disclosure. For example, if you really wanted to go out and play cards one evening, a statement like "I would really like to play cards tonight" is more appropriate than "Is it all right if I play cards tonight?"—especially if you would sit home and pout or start an argument if you received a "No" answer. Likewise the question, "Do you love me?" may be a cover-up for "I really miss you and would like you to spend more time with me." The point we are trying to make here is that some questions are truly questions ("Do you want coffee or tea with your dinner?") whereas other questions are coded messages for hidden feelings. Rather than assume that the other person will be able to decipher the coded message (remember the myth of the good friend) or will respond with the "correct" answer by chance alone, we encourage clients to state their feelings and wishes directly, with the use of a direct "I" statement.

Skill fifteen: Positive contingency contracting

Simply stated, a positive contract is a mutual exchange of rewards between two (or more) individuals who are willing to negotiate. In other words, "If you do something that I want or allow me to do something I enjoy, then I will do something that you enjoy or support you doing something that you want." There are, however, some things that are non-negotiable in working out a contract. For example, if a person wanted to take a vacation with an attractive co-worker of the opposite sex, the exchange between that person and his spouse would probably not be rewarding. In addition to negotiating for reasonable items, the contract should be fair in the sense that both parties should feel that the exchange of rewards is fairly equal. This is a very individualistic matter. Some persons, who are not assertive enough to speak up for what they feel is fair, will agree to the terms of a contract just to "keep the peace." If this occurs, the contract is likely to fail in that the person will feel cheated and will usually undermine or sabotage the agreement in some way. It should also be pointed out that there is a difference between a positive contract and a negative contract. In a positive contract, the two individuals exchange mutually agreed upon rewards; in a *negative contract,* the implication is that "If you do not do what I enjoy or allow me to do something I want to do, I will do something negative to you."

In doing assertion training we have found that the utilization of positive contingency contracting has been extremely useful in helping individuals get more of their personal needs met. One of our first objectives in assertion training is to help individuals recognize that they have personal needs, and that they should not feel guilty in wanting some of these needs to be satisfied. A second step is teaching individuals how to appropriately verbalize these needs to others. This is accomplished through discussion and behavioral rehearsal. Here again it is important that individuals learn how to make statements about what their feelings, needs, and wishes are instead of the too frequently used strategy of asking questions. Once they are able to identify and verbalize what some of their needs or wishes are without experiencing high amounts of tension and guilt, the next step is teaching them how more of these needs or wishes might be satisfied. It is at this point that positive contracting can be introduced and practiced.

In role-playing contracting situations, it is important that the person can state his feelings/needs/wishes clearly, that the person can keep his anxiety level low enough so that he hears what the other person is saying or requesting in return, and that the individual is able to say "No" to what he feels is an unfair contract. As stated previously, contracting only works if both parties are willing to listen and negotiate. When this agreement to listen and negotiate is not present, contracting may not be possible. However, our experience has been that most couples, friends, etc., are willing to engage in contracting because something positive stands to be gained for each of them. In some cases it may be necessary to make an agreement in which neither party gets exactly what he originally requested, but where more needs are satisfied than would be satisfied otherwise: If one person wanted to spend a two-week vacation fishing and the other individual wanted to spend the time shopping for antique furniture, it may be possible to pick a place where some time could be spent fishing and some time could be spent shopping.

We have used contracting rather extensively in our assertion training sessions and with homework assignments. It can be extremely valuable between husband and wife, parent and child, student and teacher, friend and friend (Homme et al., 1969; Stuart, 1969; Liberman, 1970; DeRisi & Butz, 1975). One of the advantages of negotiating and contracting is that it fosters a relationship where each person can openly communicate some of his needs rather than just criticizing the other person. In order to get what you want, you must listen to what the other person wants. We often falsely believe that we know what the other individual wants. At other times, such as in a parent-child interaction, we tend to utilize our authority position rather than negotiate a fair and honest settlement. Negotiation and contracting help to alleviate some of these problems, often drawing people closer together rather than just having them "dig in" and try to defend their wishes or desires. At times, this digging in to defend one's rights may be the only alternative; however, in most situations, especially when both parties care for one another, we have found that negotiation and contracting offer a more equitable solution.

We recognize that when one first begins to use these approach skills, they may seem awkward and stilted. However, with some effort and repeated practice, these skills can be comfortably adopted into the person's ongoing behavioral repertoire, resulting in greater need satisfaction and enhanced positive feelings. These skills may not result in a successful experience each and every time they are utilized; however, as one of the Rolling Stones' songs states, "You can't always get what you want, but if you try. . . you might find you get what you need."

10 Protective skills

Risks of protective skills

One of the most controversial issues in assertion training is the use of specific structured techniques for situations where the individual is being *unfairly* criticized, manipulated, pressured, or taken advantage of by someone else. The concerns about teaching and using these various protective skills are these:

The individual can overuse these verbal techniques to the disadvantage of the assertor and recipient—in both superficial and intimate relationships.

These structured techniques, if used alone, will not foster closer relationships between individuals.

Being the recipient of some of these protective techniques can be very frustrating.

If the assertor and the recipient do not work out a more equitable communication system and understanding, the communication and the relationship between the individuals may cease to exist as a result of using these techniques.

It is debatable as to what constitutes *unfair* criticism, pressure, manipulation, etc. By quickly turning to these procedures, the individual may become so defensive that he will not hear or respond to appropriate messages of concern.

To some extent, each of these concerns is valid; consequently, these protective techniques must be taught with a considerable amount of caution and monitoring on the part of the trainer.

Open communication

Whenever one feels that he is being treated unfairly or unjustly, a clear, honest statement of that fact is the single most assertive act a person can make. The clear, honest statement of one's needs or feelings in a relationship is the common denominator throughout all of the protective as well as the social approach procedures. It has been our experience that in most situations, an honest, clearly worded statement will be an effective and sufficient assertion. When clients ask us, "What do I say in situation X?" our reply is "What do you feel about X?" Their answer is usually the assertive communication that we encourage them to make in the situation. In our personal lives, a single, clear statement of our feelings has been the most frequently used assertive skill. As assertion trainers, we have found that facilitating clients in simply stating their feelings in any given situation consumes the majority of our efforts.

What about those individuals who do not know what they want or feel? People caught in this "existential crisis" are usually more difficult to train to be assertive. Assertion training *alone* would probably not serve their needs. However, as an assertive trainer, you must be able to discriminate between those individuals who are truly confused about their needs and those individuals who are so nonassertive that they do not feel they have a right to their values or feelings. The latter group knows what they like and dislike, but they cannot verbalize this to others. Consequently, training for this latter group involves teaching them to express feelings and needs which they have suppressed in the past.

Occasions for protective skills

Let us assume for a moment that somewhere in this vast society of ours there is a husband who does not respect his wife's self-esteem and proceeds to repeatedly call her names. Let us also assume that the wife, on several occasions, has clearly stated *to her husband*, "I feel your name-calling is very unfair to me, and I want you to stop doing this." If the husband hears her assertive response and stops, fine; but what if he disregards her message and continues the name-calling?

148

Should she begin calling him names back? Should she start crying? Should she throw something at him? Should she pack up and leave the house?

As another example, what if a door-to-door salesperson continues to high pressure you after you have clearly and assertively stated that you are not interested in buying the person's product? Do you slam the door in the individual's face? Do you make up a phony excuse? What do you do if the salesperson is already in your house? How do you handle the situation if the salesperson is a neighbor whom you know?

As a third example, how do you respond to a boss, fellow employee, relative, or friend who screams and intensely criticizes you even after you have asked this person to stop for a moment and cool off? Do you scream or criticize back? Do you attack the person physically? Do you break down and cry or become overly apologetic even before you know the issue?

There are a number of situations like these where we feel it is both appropriate and necessary to teach the client some protective skills. These are very powerful techniques which can cause a temporary or permanent break in the communication or the relationship itself. Consequently, they should only be used *after* the honest communication has failed and the other person persists in victimizing, not listening, or not respecting the client.

To some, the very idea of teaching an individual to be defensive is unacceptable. The connotation conjures up the image of an uncompromising and hostile person. However, it is important to remember that we all have and need some defenses at various times in order to survive physically and emotionally. Nonassertive individuals also have defenses. The defense may be passivity or withdrawal, it may involve the avoidance of contact with others, or the defense may be aggression. These behavior patterns do protect nonassertive/aggressive individuals, otherwise they would not be repeated over and over again.

The difficulty is that these behavior patterns are not adaptive because these individuals may end up losing their rights, friends, or personal freedom. A passive, nonassertive person is likely to have many of his needs go unsatisfied and, as a result, may be depressed with a poor self-image. The aggressive individual may get more material needs met, but the probabilities are also higher that he will not have many close and intimate friends. Hopefully, then, there are better defenses available. Another reason for teaching some protective skills stems from our experience that it is very difficult to train and motivate individuals to attempt the social approach behaviors if they are not able to also defend themselves when appropriate. In order to stick your neck out and risk being involved with people, you must also feel like you can protect yourself should someone try to hurt you.

The defensive techniques that we teach are verbal defenses which are intended to protect the individual but not insulate him from feedback and communication; one must learn to discriminate when criticism is constructive and when it is destructive. One must learn to discriminate when an angry person is angry with reason and when the anger is primarily aggressive and destructive. In superficial relationships such as a customer-salesman relationship, these decisions may be fairly easy. If the customer does not want to buy a product, he has a right not to do so. If a salesperson attempts to talk the customer out of his position after the individual has clearly stated a disinterest, a defensive technique may be appropriate to use. In personal and intimate relationships, these discriminations are more difficult to make and may initially require constant monitoring by the assertion trainer.

It is a controversial issue whether it is appropriate or constructive to give people "programmed" ways of responding to intimates when there is friction between them. We know that it is possible to train individuals to effectively shield themselves from the unfair criticisms of another. However, if these techniques are used in all situations, whether the criticism is just or unfair, the individual can become so tightly defended that no one will be able to affect the person. Closer relationships will gradually cease to exist, and the individual will perhaps remain more isolated than before.

This is a real danger. Consequently, we will once again emphasize that these protective skills are to be used only as a last resort and only after other more open, positive efforts have failed.

Terminating protective measures

Once the decision is made to use a protective technique, the individual also has the responsibility to listen for changes in the communication. If the unjust interaction is terminated, then the assertive individual should immediately cease his use of the defensive technique and resume more open communication. On the other hand, if the unjust interaction is again resumed, the defensive technique should also be repeated. Knowing when to start and when to continue using the technique is as crucial as knowing how to use it. Our experience has been that in most instances this start-stop procedure is necessary before a more equitable communication system is established. In the case of a nag, the nagging person does not immediately cease nagging. Instead the process fluctuates where the nagging ceases for awhile, then resumes, and then ceases again later. During these lulls, we feel that the honest communication should be repeated.

The primary goal in the use of these techniques is to interrupt a destructive and unjust interaction pattern, replacing it with a fair and mutually respectful communication. In our assertion groups, we encourage our clients to use negotiation and contracting as a primary tool for this. Once the destructive interaction is terminated, both parties can negotiate for a mutually satisfactory contract. In a customer-salesman relationship that may mean, as the assertor, you do not buy the product but agree to take the individual's business card for future reference. In an intimate relationship, the negotiation and contracting is usually more complex, but both parties can strive to give the other person as much as possible without negotiating away individual values, rights, and dignity.

Consequences of teaching protective skills

When these protective skills are first employed, the recipient of the interaction—the person who is doing the nagging, criticizing, pressuring—is likely to feel some frustration in not being able to affect the individual in the desired manner; consequently, the communication will probably stop. In most cases, this break in the communication system is only a temporary one and resolves itself in a more equitable interaction when the other person recognizes that the assertor is able to stand up for his rights and protect himself.

However, in some cases, the other individual may not wish to adopt a more equitable relationship. Consequently, if both individuals hold their ground, there may be a more permanent break in the relationship ultimately resulting in a divorce, loss of friendship, or loss of a job. Because of this possibility, it is very important in teaching these protective techniques that the client be aware of the possible consequences of his actions so that he *can choose* whether or not to act defensively. If, under the circumstances, the person chooses not to respond to unjust criticism with the use of verbal assertion, he may still be taught how to reduce much of the anxiety present by utilizing a procedure such as systematic desensitization.

Many individuals, however, do choose to respond when subjected to unfair circumstances. It is, perhaps, not very surprising that once individuals begin to realize that they have some rights in this world and that their own dignity need not be negotiated away, they view the termination of this inequitable relationship as a rewarding outcome rather than as a punitive consequence. It should also be noted that in many cases a more permanent break in the relationship can be avoided by working with both of the concerned parties simultaneously (e.g., husband-wife, student-teacher, child-parent, boss-employee).

In learning these protective skills, there is frequently a period in the nonassertive person's development when he begins to respond in an aggressive manner (Wolpe & Lazarus, 1966). Some of this reaction seems inevitable since the individual, perhaps for the first time in his life, is able to experience his personal power rather than being the "scapegoat" in various relationships. Consequently, there is a tendency to try out these newly acquired skills everywhere. With

152

appropriate feedback from the trainer, other group members, and individuals in the client's environment, this overreaction and testing of the limits is usually temporary and manageable. However, as a possible developmental stage, it should be anticipated by the trainer.

With all the precautions in mind, note that clients do tend to improve their appropriate assertive skills with the addition of these defensive techniques. Clients who have been trained in the use of these defensive procedures have, for the most part, maintained their previous relationships and have also established new relationships. Consequently, our experience has been that the techniques given in the following pages have been constructive rather than destructive in the client's relationships with others. With practice comes the sophistication to be able to appropriately and fairly discriminate when to use and when not to use the protective techniques. The assertor will have much lower anxiety in these situations; consequently, he will be less likely to distort what is being said and will be less likely to hear an "attack" statement where one is not intended. With practice and sophistication, the assertor will have less need to resort to a "protective shield" and, instead, will rely more heavily on open, honest, and clear communication.

As a final note we would like to point out that in observing and reading about others who are doing assertion training, we sometimes find that an inordinate amount of time is spent in teaching the client how to put off others and to protect himself. Although we feel that this is an important and necessary part of the assertion training process, we also feel that a greater amount of time should be spent teaching the individual how to foster closer, more meaningful relationships. It is perhaps true that before an individual is willing and able to get very close to another person, he first must feel able to protect himself. However, defenses alone are not enough. As John Stevens (1971, p. 34) stated, *"The walls that keep out arrows and spears also keep out kisses and roses."* Teaching the protective skills alone or almost exclusively is not conducive to the overall goals of assertion training. Instead, it is of the utmost importance to remember that building greater self-esteem and closer, more mutually pleasurable relationships is the ultimate goal of assertion training.

With these cautions as an introduction, we will now describe some specific techniques with which individuals can protect themselves from being taken advantage of by others when the situation calls for this. These protective skills include broken record, selective ignoring, disarming anger, sorting issues, guilt reduction, and apologies. Fog and negative inquiry are two additional techniques which we will present to provide historical perspective; however, we have dropped teaching the use of the fog because of its strong passive-aggressive flavor and because it requires the individual to say something he does not really believe. We have also dropped negative inquiry because of the strong self-concept demands placed upon the assertor.

As can be readily noticed, some of the techniques are similar in their content and their purpose. Which technique is chosen is often a matter of personal style. In some cases, one or more techniques can be combined and used simultaneously in the interaction. Here again the advantage of multiple therapists is evident in that each of us often prefers to use a different technique or a combination of techniques under similar circumstances. By discussing, modeling, and practicing each of these techniques, the client is better able to evaluate and adopt that approach which best fits his particular personality and the circumstances of the situation.

Protection one: Broken record

Of the various protective techniques used, the broken record is probably the most basic. The broken record can be used by itself, or as a component of several of the other techniques to follow. In addition to being potentially useful in situations where a person is defending himself from being nagged, criticized, or pressured, the broken record can also be used in situations where the assertor is requesting something for himself.

The broken record is essentially the continuous repetition of the clear statement of the assertor's feelings or main

154

point. No other issues are attended to in the conversation other than the point being made by the assertor. In effect, the individual sounds like a "broken record," repeating over and over again his position in as concise a statement as possible. In many conversations, side issues are brought in by the other individual to distract or anger the person. To respond to these side issues can escalate the conversation to the point where all clarity of the main point is lost. With the use of the broken record, one point is covered at a time and all side issues are saved for later discussions.

In a superficial relationship such as a customer-salesperson interaction, responding to the salesperson's side issues and questions gives the salesperson (S) more information to use toward selling the product to the customer (C).

S: I would like to show you some great magazines which I am selling.

C: No thank you, I'm not interested in buying any magazines today.

S: Do you have any children?

C: Yes.

S: Well, we have some very educational and enjoyable children's magazines to offer.

C: They have all the magazines they need.

S: As an interested parent you could provide them with magazines that would increase their motivation to learn. How are they doing in school?

C: They are doing pretty well in school except for math.

At this point the salesperson is well on the way to controlling the conversation and, perhaps, the outcome of the interaction. By focusing on the customer's children, the salesperson may be able to arouse enough guilt or interest to make a sale. If the customer's children are having some difficulty in school, or if the salesperson can get the potential customer to make other disclosures about himself or his family, then the salesperson will be more likely to make a sale. Let us take this conversation again, only this time we will utilize the protective shield of the broken record *after* the clear, honest communication does not terminate the interaction.

S: I would like to show you some great magazines which I am selling.

C: No thank you, I am not interested in buying any magazines today. (Honest and clear communication.)

S: We really have some great magazines to offer.

C: That may be quite true, but I have all the magazines I want to read. (Honest and clear communication.)

S: Do you have any children?

C: The point is I'm not interested in buying any magazines today. (Broken record.)

S: Well then, is your wife home? She may be interested.

C: I don't want any magazines. (Broken record.)

S: Wouldn't you like her to make her own choice on that, sir?

C: I don't want any magazines. (Broken record.)

Note: The customer is choosing not to answer the questions. There is nothing blazed in the sky that says we have to answer all questions asked of us.

S: Sir, have I told you that one-half of the profits in these sales go to medical research. Aren't you concerned about your health or the future health of your children?

C: The point is I'm not interested in any magazines. (Broken record.)

S: OK, OK. Would you at least take this brochure and think about it?

C: Yes, I will take the brochure. (Negotiated ending.)

S: Thank you.

C: You're welcome.

156

The conversation here was quite different from the previous interaction. With the broken record, no free information was given nor were side issues attended to. The customer's interest in medical research was irrelevant to his interest in not purchasing magazines. The salesperson in this situation did not attend to the original clear statement of the customer, and it was necessary to repeat the statement until the salesperson did finally get the message. Notice that towards the end of the interaction, the salesperson tried to negotiate for something in his behalf—taking the brochure—which the customer accepted. The customer, in this case, may choose to think about buying magazines at a later date or may immediately discard the brochure. However it was an attempt to leave the salesperson feeling like he did accomplish something with his potential customer.

In the previous example, the broken record was being used where the assertor was refusing or saying "No" to someone. This technique can also be effectively and appropriately used in situations where the assertor is making a request. The procedure is the same as before. The assertor returns the conversation to the main point whenever irrelevant issues are introduced or he is being ignored. The person using the broken record does not necessarily repeat the same sentence over and over again. As long as the conversation is on the relevant topic, there is no reason to restate the original sentence. If, on the other hand, a side issue is brought up, the original sentence stating one's position is then repeated.

Because conversation continues and negotiation and contracting are possible using this technique, the other person is not as likely to become frustrated. Also, this technique is not necessarily intended to end a conversation as some of the other protective techniques are designed to do. In the following example, our mythical hero, Sherwin (S), will attempt to get our mythical villain, Julio (J), to commit himself to an important writing deadline using the broken record.

S: Hi, I want to talk to you about setting a deadline for the writing of our book. (Clear and honest communication.)

J: Sherwin, it's the weekend; let's go sailing.

S: Julio, we need to set a deadline date. (Broken record.)

J: Oh, Sherwin, you always nag, nag, nag.

S: Let's set a date for our deadline and then we can talk about other things. (Broken record and negotiation offer.)

J: I haven't got my appointment book.

S: Where is it at?

J: Downstairs in the car.

S: Please go get it so we can finish this up. (Broken record.)

J: I'll do it later.

S: Julio we have been putting this off for weeks now. Please go get your appointment book so we can set a deadline. (Broken record.)

J: OK, I'll go get it. Then can we talk about sailing?

S: Sure, after we agree on some writing time. (Contract.)

J: I'll be back in a moment. (Leaves to get his appointment book.)

The conversation here did continue, and neither party attempted to terminate the interaction without reaching an agreement. The negotiation and contracting began with both of them agreeing to consider sailing after the deadline was set. When Julio returned from the car, a deadline date may have been easily agreed upon, or Sherwin may have had to resort to the broken record throughout the conversation in order to come to an agreement.

In using the broken record and the other protective skills to follow, there are two important points to remember. First of all, if you are defending yourself using one of these techniques, it may be necessary to stay with the technique for several responses until the other individual gets tired and begins to back off. Although you may be able to stop a negative interaction with just one broken record response, the likelihood is that you will need to use this protective shield at least three times in succession before the other person stops. In some cases you will need more than three responses; consequently, we have our clients practice giving eight to twelve responses in order to overlearn this defensive stance. In most cases, however, about three responses will do it. As an example, one large encyclopedia company instructs its door-to-door salespeople to break off the sales pitch if the potential customer says "No" three times without giving any extra information to work on.

Secondly, if you are asking for some need of yours to be filled (e.g., asking someone next to you to put out a cigarette that is bothering you), you must be prepared to make the request at least two times. It is amazing how many requests are turned down on asking the first time and then agreed to on the second request. It is recognized that just making the request is a very important first step for a nonassertive individual and that this alone can do much to enhance his self-image and dignity. However, as the individual becomes more confident in his assertive skills, further encouragement should be given to make the request at least a second time before assuming that nothing will be done by the other person.

Protection two: Selective ignoring

Selective ignoring is the discriminatory attending and nonattending to specific content from another individual. That is, the assertor does not reply to unfair or abusive interactions, but instead replies only to statements that are not destructive, guilt-producing, or unjust. The verbally abusive individual is met with silence when he is being unjust. Not only does the assertor remain totally silent through the unfair interactions, but his nonverbal cues must also be controlled. Head-nodding in particular is a reinforcing, nonverbal cue to a speaker. Those who have had public speaking experience will recall how comfortable it is to speak to an audience that is smiling and head-nodding in approval. The rationale for the effectiveness of this technique is that the assertor extinguishes the responses of the other person. That is, the assertor no longer resists the interaction, but simply removes the reinforcement. This technique is relatively easy to use under high anxiety states in that it requires no defensive speech. However, the effectiveness of the technique involves sophisticated discriminations of when to attend and when not to attend to specific information. The assertor does try to continue an ongoing conversation, but responds selectively to the information given.

When training this skill in our groups, we usually begin with a simulated phone conversation. The role-playing clients sit back-to-back and speak through an imaginary phone. The seating arrangements and the phone conversation are used to eliminate nonverbal cues. The clients can then concentrate entirely on the verbal discriminations. After clients have become proficient with the phone conversation arrangement, then face-to-face conversations are attempted. Visual aids such as a mirror or videotape can be extremely helpful here in aiding the client to control body movements.

As an example of where a selective ignoring procedure can be effectively used, imagine a situation where a daughter (D) is getting a phone call from a guilt-producing and nagging mother (M).

D: Hello.

M: Hi, precious, how are you?

D: Oh, hi Mom. I'm fine, how are you?

M: Now that you ask, I am not very good.

D: Oh, that's too bad, what's the matter?

M: You never call us anymore now that you are out living on your own. I guess you are just too busy for your parents.

D: Mom, you know I still love you and Dad very much. However, what with working, going to school, and trying to pay all of my own expenses, calling you long-distance more than once a week is just too much for me. (Clear and honest communication.)

M: Are you saying we are not worth the price of a phone call or that you cannot take a couple of minutes to call us every other day? After all, there is no one left in the house anymore except Dad and me.

D: Mother, I really don't want to continue talking like this. I feel that you are unfairly criticizing me again, and when conversations like this continue, we only end up arguing. I am not going to respond to your criticisms if you continue. How's Dad? (Honest communication with an alternative topic being offered.)

M: I only criticize you for your own good. After all, I wouldn't expect some of those people you call your friends to say anything.

D: (Silence.)

M: Are you still dating that bum Pete?

D: (Silence.)

M: I asked if you were still dating that bum Pete?

D: (Silence.)

M: Hello, are you still there?

D: Yes, Mother, I am still here.

M: Why aren't you answering me then?

D: Mom, I said I do not like the constant criticism. I feel that I am old enough to make decisions and choices as to whom I date. (Clear and honest communication.)

M: Well, if that were true, you would be married by now. After all, how many girls are still unmarried and going to school at the age of thirty-one?

D: (Silence.)

M: Are you silent because you do not have a good answer to that question?

D: (Silence.)

M: Well, if you are not going to answer my questions, what is there left to talk about? (Offer of negotiation.)

D: Would you like to hear about my promotion at work? (Return offer.)

M: Oh, you got a promotion. Tell me about it. (Acceptance.)

Depending upon the mother's response, it may be necessary for the daughter to give a number of silences (i.e., selective ignoring) before a more pleasant topic of conversation ensues. If the nagging interaction pattern between the mother and daughter is a longstanding one, a single phone conversation using the selective ignoring procedure will probably not change the situation very much. The next time mother calls, the old pattern will probably repeat itself. In time, however, some permanent change may occur: The mother will continue talking with the daughter, but will be much less critical. However, an immediate change which can occur is that the daughter need not either agree or argue with everything the mother says. By not responding to all of the mother's questions and criticisms, the daughter can enjoy some relief from the stressful, guilt-producing conversation.

The selective ignoring technique (or, for that matter, any of the other defensive techniques) does not guarantee a change in the other person's behavior, even though this is often the result. These techniques are intended to protect the recipient of an unjust interaction. A high pressure salesperson, for example, may remain a high pressure salesperson; he simply will not be able to sell to more assertive clients.

Protection three: Disarming anger

Disarming anger can be an extremely useful protective technique—in some cases, it may even save the person's life. This technique involves an honest contract offered by the assertor to another individual who is exhibiting high amounts of anger and who may, in fact, be bordering on physical violence. The contract that the assertor tries to work out is an agreement stating that the assertor will talk about what-

162

ever issue the other person wants, but only after some of his anger dissipates. Essentially, this is a negotiation for a cooling off period so that both parties can think more clearly and hopefully resolve the issue at hand. This contract is offered whether or not the accusations being made are true or false. Even if the accusations are true and the assertor does eventually apologize, there is no reason why this individual should be made to look or feel like a worthless, stupid human being in the process (or be physically assaulted). As part of the technique, the assertor does not reply to name-calling or other side issues. The assertor also does not escalate the interaction by screaming back. In effect, he uses a broken record offering the contract, "I will talk about whatever you want, but first calm down." In this case the assertor must be able to sit patiently through the individual's initial bursts of anger. (In extreme cases when one's physical safety is at stake, getting away from the situation for awhile may be a wiser choice if this is possible.) It is also important that the assertor is able to appear reasonably relaxed throughout this part of the interaction; consequently, as part of the training procedure, it may be necessary to desensitize the client to screaming as well as to the anger in the screaming.

Disarming anger is not intended to negate or invalidate the other individual's anger. The intention is to use the technique in order to facilitate communication—not to terminate it. We feel that whenever a person's anger is very high, his ability to listen and incorporate new information is diminished. Trying to talk with such an angry person can be frustrating, useless, and risky. If some technique is not used here, the danger exists that both individuals will become extremely angry—possibly to the point where verbal or physical abuse is escalated. Although some anger and a raised voice may be very appropriate at times, we believe that people have the right not to be abused by extreme anger regardless of the reason: The intent of this technique is to disarm *extreme, unreasonable* anger. Although many constructive communications can be made in anger (Bach & Wyden, 1968), for this to occur the fighting must be "fair," where communication is honest, direct, and specific; where name-calling is eliminated;

where issues are not stored; and where the ultimate aim is to clear the air rather than to emerge as the "winner."

Disarming anger can be a useful addition to a person's ability to cope with other people. As an example of this technique, imagine there is an angry, irrational boss (B) screaming at our mild-mannered assertor named Tim (T).

B: (Screaming) Tim, you did it again. You are so stupid. When are you going to learn to get your paperwork done on time? Now I'm in trouble because you didn't do your job.

T: You are really angry. I'm not sure what paperwork you're talking about. Why don't you sit down so we can talk about it. (Clear and honest communication.)

B: Talk about it! I'm not sure you're smart enough to listen to a simple sentence in English. Now, damn it, I want you to do your work.

T: (Calmly) As I said, I want to talk to you about all this, but I really don't like to be screamed at. Sit down and let's try to talk about it calmly. (Clear and honest communication.)

B: I am calm, you idiot! Can't you do anything right?

T: I would like to talk with you about it, but only if we can go over it calmly. I really get uncomfortable with your screaming. (Technique begins here.)

B: I am surprised an idiot like you is capable of having any feelings.

T: I will be willing to talk to you about the paperwork if you will sit down and stop screaming.

B: What if I don't want to stop screaming?

T: Then let's talk about this whole matter later today when you are not so angry. I want to get this thing settled too, but only if you are not screaming at me. (Negotiation offer.)

B: I want to settle this thing now.

T: Then please sit down and stop screaming so we can do this.

B: OK. I'm sitting and I am not screaming. Why didn't you do your work?

At this point it appears that Tim has managed to disarm some of the boss' anger. The boss still has to communicate what paperwork Tim did not do, and Tim still has to account for his actions. It could be that the work actually was done, but trying to discuss the matter while the anger is so intense would be very difficult. However, once the boss is willing to sit down and talk about the matter more calmly, there is a greater likelihood that the situation can be discussed and, hopefully, resolved. Also note that in the above interaction, Tim chose not to take issue with the name-calling, but instead focused his attention on the boss' anger and screaming. At a later time when the boss is not as enraged, it may be quite appropriate for Tim to communicate that name-calling tends to hamper his relationship with the boss.

Protection four: Sorting issues

Occasionally, in the course of an interaction, more than one message or issue will become sandwiched together. Unless these issues or messages are sorted out and dealt with separately, the individual may begin to feel confused, anxious, and guilty. Consequently, it is to the assertor's and the recipient's advantage to deal with these different issues separately. Consider the following interaction between Bonnie (B) and Dorothy (D).

B: Dorothy, my car is in the garage again. Will you drive me into Beverly Hills tomorrow so that I can visit my cousin?

D: Normally, I would be glad to drive you, but I have already made plans to go on a picnic tomorrow with the family. (Clear and honest communication.)

B: Dorothy, I don't ask you for favors very often.

165

D: I realize that, Bonnie, but I just will not be able to make it tomorrow. How about my taking you next week? (Negotiation.)

B: By then I will probably have my own car back and will not need you. I thought you were a friend I could count on for help.

D: Bonnie, I hope I am still your friend, and that I can help you at times. However, I will not be able to drive you into Beverly Hills tomorrow.

B: If I were really your friend, then you would take me.

D: Again, I do consider you my friend, Bonnie, but I think the issue here is whether or not I will be able to drive you into Beverly Hills tomorrow.

An attempt was made to sort the issue of friendship from being available as a driver. Oftentimes, when two or more issues are sandwiched together and are not properly sorted, the individual goes away feeling guilty or anxious. By attempting to sort the various issues at hand, the assertor is better able to discriminate just what is being asked or implied by the other individual so that he can then formulate an appropriate response without leaving things unresolved or "up in the air."

Sorting issues is a more complex procedure to practice because more verbal response may be required than with some of the other techniques. Situations that can benefit from this procedure typically occur less frequently, and the sandwiching of different issues may be more subtle than overt criticism, nagging, or anger: "If you loved me, then you would. . . ." "I thought you appreciated the favor I did for you—how could you. . . ." "Don't you care about this job? Why is it you. . . ." However, when the need does arise for sorting issues, we have found this procedure to be very useful.

Protection five: Guilt reduction and the No "I'm Sorry" Rule

We approach the reduction of personal guilt from both a didactic and behavioral direction. Guilt is a frequently reported feeling by many of the people with whom we work. It is true that, during the course of our lives, we become dependent upon a number of other individuals in order to satisfy many of our physical and emotional needs. As children, we are dependent upon our parents or on some other adult for our food, shelter, and attention. As adolescents we become dependent upon our peers for approval. As adults we may be dependent upon others for love, support, physical safety, or our jobs. It is little wonder then that when we go against the wishes of these "significant others" who are satisfying some of our basic needs we begin to feel uncomfortable. In a sense, we have a responsibility to others. But we also have a responsibility to ourselves. Our responsibility to others involves being open and honest without violating their dignity; it does not include always pleasing them.

With individuals who are unnecessarily experiencing guilt, we make every supportive comment we can think of in order for them to find some strength and responsibility that lies within them: the strength to experience new things and grow, the strength to express their feelings, the strength to do things in a manner which they feel is best for them and which does not violate the rights (but not necessarily the wishes) of others, and the responsibility to accept this strength and freedom as theirs and theirs alone. Individuals who are experiencing high amounts of guilt need support to validate that they are meaningful human beings who are entitled to certain rights and needs of their own, even when these rights and needs apparently conflict with the desires of some other significant person in their lives. Hopefully, this support can be found in every assertion training group.

In addition to this verbal support, we utilize a No "I'm Sorry" Rule in our assertion training groups. This rule states that no one, including trainers and aggressive clients, can use the specific words "I'm sorry" during the group period.

Individuals with undue amounts of guilt *often* find themselves telling others that they are sorry for doing or not doing something. Frequently they do not stop to consider the possibility that their actions may have been appropriate in the situation or that nothing wrong was really done to merit an

"I'm sorry" response. Instead, they say "I'm sorry" almost automatically.

If the "I'm sorry" statement is made during the session, it is pointed out to the individual, and he is asked to rephrase the statement without using these words. In cases where the individual feels there is no reason to apologize for his actions, he is encouraged, and coached if necessary, to repeat the statement without using the words "I'm sorry." If, in fact, the individual does feel an apology of some sort is in order, he is asked to rephrase the response and give an apology without using the specific words "I'm sorry." For example, let's assume that one of the clients (C) comes in twenty minutes late to the group therapy session and the trainer (T) reacts in the following way.

T: You are late.

C: Yes, I know. I'm sorry.

T: I feel it is very important that we all start these sessions on time—together.

C: I said I am sorry.

If this situation did occur, the client would be asked if he felt there was a good reason for being late. If the answer was "No," and if the client felt an apology was in order, he might be coached to handle the situation by admitting his error but without compromising his own dignity.

T: You are late.

C: Yes, I know. I apologize for being late, but I did not realize how late it was when I left the house.

T: I do not like excuses. I feel it is very important that we all start these sessions on time—together.

C: It was not intended as an excuse. I was just telling you what happened. I will try to be here on time next week.

If, on the other hand, the client felt there was a good reason for being late, he would be coached to handle the situation differently. For example:

T: You are late.

C: Yes, I know. I had something come up which was very important and which I felt I had to attend to before I came here.

Note: The person need not go into the reason for being late unless he wishes to do so.

T: Isn't the group important to you? Besides, you kept the rest of us waiting.

C: Yes the group is important to me, and my intent was not to keep the rest of the group waiting; however, I did want to attend to this other matter first.

T: Just what was so important that you had to do?

C: I appreciate your interest, but I do not wish to go into it right now. You will have to trust me that I felt it was important enough for me to be late to group. I will try to be here on time next week.

T: What if something comes up again next week?

C: Again, I can only repeat to you that the group is important to me, and that I will try to be here on time. However, if something does come up again next week, I will have to make the decision then as to what I feel I should do first.

T: If you make it a habit of coming in late, we will have to consider dropping you from the group. Especially, when you do not tell us why you were late.

C: I can see that you feel coming to group on time is very important, and I have no intention of making this a steady habit. However, just as you must have priorities in life, I do too, and I hope that you will be able to respect and trust my decision for coming in late today even if I do not wish to discuss what that reason involved.

In the above example, we have portrayed the therapist as taking a very rigid role (at least, it is not what one would call "unconditional positive regard"). We may actually play this role in group in order to give the client some practice in dealing with such individuals. The important point here is that the client would be carefully coached as to how to handle a situation such as this without sacrificing self-respect and without saying, "I'm sorry," when in fact he felt there was a good reason for being late.

We recognize that there is nothing magical in the words "I'm sorry." But they are used too often by individuals when they do not really mean to apologize or when they feel excessive amounts of guilt. As such, we impose the No "I'm Sorry" Rule in order to overcome these situations.

Protection six: Apologies

As assertion trainers we believe that some feelings of guilt may be appropriate in some situations. When an individual feels badly for being disrespectful or abusive to another individual and subsequently makes an apology, we believe this is a legitimate action. In this case, the bad feeling (i.e., guilt) experienced by the abusive individual may help him avoid being abusive in the future. The apology, in turn, gives some validation to the other person's feelings and lets this person know that the abusive individual is aware of what happened. An individual who never apologizes or admits ill treatment to another will probably experience some difficulty in forming close interpersonal relationships. Likewise, individuals who are repeatedly hurt by another will tend to avoid ongoing interactions with this abusive person in the future.

We have encountered individuals who make very few apologies. Frequently, these individuals feel that by making an apology they will end up in a "one-down" position where their self-esteem will be damaged or where others will then begin to take unfair advantage of them. On the other end of the continuum are those individuals who, in order to avoid being criticized by others, make an excessive number of apologies even when these apologies are not warranted. With both types of individuals, we attempt to teach the skill of making appropriate apologies without sacrificing one's self-esteem or dignity.

Essentially, in teaching individuals how to apologize, we work on apologizing for the behavior that was abusive to the other person without communicating that the person who is making the apology is generally hurtful or unworthy. In effect, the individual making the apology asserts that his self-worth is not measured by one example of an inappropriate behavior. The skill of apologizing may involve a number of other protective skills such as sorting issues or disarming anger when the recipient of the apology is feeling hurt or angry. In such cases, the individual making the apology must be prepared to stay with the situation until these other feelings are resolved and until the initial message can be heard, as in the following interaction between Nick (N) and Ruth (R).

N: You look upset; is something bothering you?

R: Yes, I am sick and tired of your constant neglect and lack of concern for me.

N: I don't understand what you are talking about.

R: Last night when we went out with Tom and Carol, you spent the whole evening talking about what you do with everyone else in the world. Not once did you mention me or some of the things we do. I am not someone you really care for, but just an appendage to your life that you utilize at your convenience.

N: I did not realize that you felt so left out of everything last night. If I excluded you from most of my conversations, it was certainly unintentional. Looking back on the situation, I agree with you. I was inconsiderate and I apologize. (The apology.)

R: The fact that you left me out of everything just shows how little I mean to you.

N: Ruth, I said I apologize for leaving you out of the conversations so much last night. However, I do not think that automatically means I do not care for you—the fact

171

is that I care a great deal about you. (Apology and sorting of issues.)

R: You're selfish, you're egotistical, and you don't give a damn about anyone but yourself.

N: I can understand that you are feeling angry and hurt; however, I don't believe all of those accusations are true because of my neglect for you last night.

Note that Nick chose here to sort issues again rather than possibly escalate the interaction by responding to the abusive name-calling in a like manner.

R: Maybe we should call it quits. Who needs you anyway?

N: Ruth, I want you to hear that you do mean a great deal to me, and that I do care about your feelings. (Open, honest communication.)

R: If what you say is true, how come you paid so little attention to me last night?

N: As I said, I did not realize I was excluding you so much. I was very interested in what Tom and I were talking about, and I did not realize that you were feeling hurt and left out. In the future, I will try to be more aware of your needs when we go out with someone else. (Restatement of apology and negotiation for future change.)

R: OK, but don't let it happen again.

N: I will try to see that it does not happen again, but at the same time, I would like you to express your feelings at the time rather than getting angry with the situation and telling me the next day.

R: That sounds fair. I'll try to communicate my feelings sooner if you try to include me more often in your conversations with others.

N: Agreed. Now are there some other issues or feelings that we should try to clear up?

R: No, I think that was the issue I was angry about. Let's see how things go for awhile and then talk about the situation again later.

N: Did you hear what I said earlier about how important you are to me?

R: Yes, I heard that, and I think that is what I need to hear more often.

N: I need to hear those things too, so maybe things will work out better the next time.

In ending this interaction, Nick has not only been able to express an apology, sort some issues, and disarm some anger, but he has also been able to express one of his own needs while maintaining his own dignity.

Protection seven: Fog

Of all the defensive techniques, the fog is probably the most controversial. The reason for this is that the fog is a passive-aggressive technique in which the individual takes on an extremely passive role in the interaction. It is not a difficult technique to learn; consequently, it was originally used with hospitalized individuals and with those who were experiencing high levels of anxiety.

The term "fog" was coined as a metaphorical description of the individual's stance in the interaction. The assertor using the fog appears to agree that the other individual, *"may be right"* or that he *"is probably correct."* The assertor does not specifically state that the other person is correct, but only that he *may* be correct. Likewise, the assertor never agrees that he will change. This technique can be especially effective in interrupting a chronic nag. For example, follow this brief interaction where Richard (R) is nagging Sarah (S) about her driving. Sarah attempts to first give the assertive clear communication, and, when that fails, she begins using the fog.

R: Sarah, you are really driving poorly again. I've asked you a million times not to drive that way.

S: We have been through this before, Richard. You know I don't appreciate it when you are so constantly critical of my driving. After all, you did ask me to take you into Los Angeles today. (Clear and honest communication.)

R: But Sarah, I am only telling you these things for your own good. Careful, you are coming much too close to the cars in front of you.

S: Richard, I would like you to stop criticizing. I feel I am driving safely. I have never had an accident or a ticket for reckless driving. (Clear and honest communication.)

R: Look at you. You look at me when you talk and take your eyes off the road. You shouldn't have your radio on either because it probably distracts you.

S: You're probably right, Richard, I shouldn't have the radio on. (Begins the fog here.)

R: Then you agree, you are a reckless driver!

S: You may be right. (Fog.)

R: Don't glance in my direction when you talk to me.

S: (Glancing in his direction) You're probably right, Richard, I shouldn't look your way. (Fog.)

R: But you are still doing it. Why are you saying I may be right?

S: Richard, I am not really agreeing with you, I just don't want to be nagged anymore. Let's talk about something else. (Clear and honest communication.)

At this point Richard may or may not respond to the last communication given to him by Sarah. Sarah may have to resume the fog, or she may be able to negotiate another solution.

Fog has proven to be an effective tool against unfair, nagging criticism. The behavioral rationale is that if you resist and try to fight back with a nagging person, you are attending to and, thereby, reinforcing the nagging behavior. The fog (a stance of offering no resistance and yet being immovable) is an attempt to remove the reinforcement from the interaction and to cause the behavior to extinguish. At the same time, however, the fog is both a dishonest and passive-aggressive communication system in the sense that the individual is saying something he does not really believe or mean. He also has no intention of changing the behavior in question, even though the recipient of the fog may be lead to believe this. Because of this objection, we have dropped this technique from our assertion training procedures.

Protection eight: Critical inquiry

Critical inquiry is a defensive technique which is sometimes effective when an individual is being unjustly criticized, knows this criticism is unjust, and has a strong positive self-image. Since the heart of this technique is to ask for more criticism, the individual must be able to hear criticism without becoming phobic or internalizing these comments. When the individual is not able to avoid internalizing these criticisms, then the technique is not advisable. When criticism begins, the assertor listens attentively and then gives a clear and honest assertive statement that he would like the criticism to cease. If the criticism continues, the assertor simply asks if there is anything else that the individual does not like. The assertor does not defend any specific criticism or counter one criticism with another. His typical reply is "Is there anything else you don't like?"

The behavioral rationale for critical inquiry is one of satiation, whereas selective ignoring and the fog relate more to an extinction paradigm. That is, if the critic finds criticizing reinforcing, then allowing that behavior to continue at a high rate for an extended period of time will, theoretically, tend to satiate and stop the criticism. Like the individual who eats so many candy bars that he cannot bear the sight of another, it is anticipated that the critic will eventually get tired of his own criticisms (besides, the critic is having to do all of the work). During this time, the assertive individual must be prepared to patiently listen to these criticisms without internalizing or trying to defend the negative comments.

As an example of this technique, consider the following interaction where John (J) is commenting on Larry's (L) clothing.

J: Larry, how many times do I have to tell you that you are a slob?

L: John, we have gone through this on a number of occasions. I really like how I look, and others whom I have asked for an opinion generally agree with my taste in clothes. I have decided I do not want to change, so let's not talk about this now. (Clear and honest communication.)

J: You really shouldn't wear a high-neck T-shirt with a sport shirt, Larry. The T-shirt shows through the open collar. You look very unprofessional.

L: I really don't want to talk about this. (Clear and honest communication.)

J: I am doing it for your own good.

L: OK, John, you don't like my T-shirt. Is there anything else you don't like about the way I dress? (Critical inquiry.)

J: As a matter of fact there is. You have white tennis shoes on with your dark brown suit. Larry, at least wear some dark shoes, preferably ones without holes.

L: You don't like my shoes. Is there anything else? (Critical inquiry.)

J: Larry, don't you know that brown pants don't go well with your bright red socks?

L: Is there anything else you don't like? (Critical inquiry.)

After five more minutes of pointing out to Larry that his camping knife on his rope belt doesn't go too well with his plaid sport jacket and that he is not dressed appropriately to speak at the psychological convention, John would hopefully become tired of listening to "Is there anything else you don't like?"

J: No Larry, I just hope someday you will listen to me.

L: OK, John, if I do decide to re-evaluate my dress, I will come to you for your advice. Until then would you agree not to bring up the subject again? (Attempt to contract.)

J: I'll really try. Are you serious that you may come to me for advice?

L: Yes. (Honest communication.)

J: That makes me feel better.

Our past experience with this technique is that it can be effective; however, it takes an individual with a very strong positive self-concept to carry it off without feeling abused and angry in the process. In that most of the individuals who seek some assertion training do not feel comfortable in eliciting repeated criticisms from others, negative inquiry has not proven to be as successful as a clear, open message of dissatisfaction or as successful as some of the other previously mentioned protective skills. For that reason, we have dropped the use of critical inquiry for most of our clients.

We have included the fog and critical inquiry because we did at one time (unwisely) advocate their general use, and because we know of others who are utilizing these procedures and may not be aware of the inherent dangers these two procedures hold for individuals and for interpersonal relationships.

11 Homework assignments

Rationale

It is our opinion that much of the success in doing assertion training stems from the homework assignments that are given. In addition to impressing the group members with our creative brilliance for thinking up clever things for them to do between the training sessions, the homework assignments accomplish several important functions.

To begin with, if the homework assignments are timed properly and geared to the individual's ability level, they can provide observable and successful experiences in functioning assertively. These experiences may be extremely important in beginning to reverse the individual's poor self-image and belief that he has little influence over his environment. During the course of a week, approximately 112 hours are spent awake and approximately 56 hours are spent sleeping. If only one or two of these waking hours are spent doing therapy, it is little wonder why clients sometimes complain that it takes years before they are able to see any observable changes in their lives.

Secondly, homework assignments help to generalize what has been practiced and learned in the group to the outside world. Because a client is able to be assertive within the group, this does not necessarily mean that he will be assertive outside of the group. The difficulty is that people can and do learn to discriminate the difference between their treatment setting and their daily environment. This was found to occur in Guerra's (1971) study where stutterers undergoing speech therapy in only a clinical setting were not as fluent in their work, school, or home environments unless their treatment was also carried out in these outside environments. Also, in an assertion training study by McFall & Lillesand (1971), it was found that some generalization of training did occur, but only in respect to the refusal situations practiced in the training and not to other assertive response styles which were not practiced during the course of treatment. Consequently, by giving frequent and varied homework assignments, we are trying to increase the probability that these newly acquired skills will be successfully used outside of the group, and that these varied experiences will enable the individual to adapt to different unexpected assertive situations in the future.

Initial assignments

The first assignments given are relatively simple ones where the client is most likely to have a low anxiety level and, at the same time, meet with some success. These first assignments may include activities such as reading a book related to assertion issues (e.g., *Your Perfect Right, The Assertive Woman, How to be Your Own Best Friend*), listening to audio tape cassettes describing assertion training and providing modeled examples of various assertive skills (Guerra & Cotler, 1975), practicing eye contact with someone on TV, or listening for free information in someone else's conversation.

If the client fails to carry out some of these early assignments where the anxiety level has been determined to be very low, one might seriously question his willingness to carry out more difficult assignments in future sessions. When failure to complete assignments repeatedly occurs, we will talk with the client and indicate that assertion training involves a commitment to work on assertive issues both during the group *and* outside of the group. In most cases, a strongly worded comment such as this is enough to motivate the person to practice outside assignments and keep appropriate records.

We make these assignments simple because we want to insure some initial success, we want the individual to become accustomed to filling out the various Assertive Data Collection Package record sheets, and we want to start the person at the low end of his assertive hierarchy.

Recording

The record sheets are extremely useful in assertion training; however, in that most individuals have not been previously trained to keep accurate behavioral records, it is necessary to teach this skill early in the assertion training process. By taking the time to do this with some of the earlier and simpler assignments, we find we are able to accomplish this function much easier. At the same time, we can begin collecting data on specific situations (using the Homework Diary, the Assertion Training Diary, and the Assertive Goal Scale), which can then be used for discussion and practice within the session.

Starting points

Before individuals are asked to carry out contracting with a spouse, close friend, or boss, they are first asked to demonstrate their ability to get some simpler needs met in other more superficial relationships. (This is assuming that the more intimate relationships are causing them comparatively more difficulty.) Consequently, before we would ask the client to engage in contracting with a spouse or boss, we would first make certain through the homework assignments that he could carry out tasks such as asking a gas station attendant for some special service (e.g., check battery water) or requesting a special table at a restaurant. Only after the client is able to demonstrate that he can get some of these needs met in a less stressful situation would we ask him to engage in something more intricate like a lengthy discussion for personal needs with a spouse, boss, or close friend.

There may be a "behavioral lag" between successful assertive behaviors in the group and what individuals can accomplish successfully in the environment outside of the group. Although we try to simulate the real-life situation as much as possible in the behavioral rehearsal, the stimulus cues can never be matched exactly. Consequently, it is not surprising that there is not a one-to-one correlation between what a person can accomplish with low anxiety within the group and what can be done outside of the group. As a result, the homework assignment often calls for a behavior that is lower on the hierarchy than what has just been completed in group. For example, let's assume an individual is working on direct eye contact in the group and, for the first time, is able to role-play a conversation using good eye contact and maintaining a SUDS level of 20. The first homework assignment then may be to practice longer conversations using primarily indirect eye contact (i.e., looking at the other person's forehead) and to use direct eye contact only with people he passes on the street or talks to for a very short period of time (e.g., a service station attendant). Only after successfully role-playing the conversation in the group several more times with good eye contact and low SUDS would he be assigned this homework task outside of the group.

While it is extremely important that the individual receive praise and support for his efforts as well as for his successful assertive behaviors, it is also important that the failures are discussed and, if possible, role-played and coached several times before any subsequent homework assignments are given in this area. This lessens the probability of similar failures occurring again in the future. Reviewing the Homework Diary during the group not only tends to increase the probability that the individual will be assertive in the future, but it can serve as an excellent learning model for others in the group as well. Going over the homework assignments and these record sheets is usually one of the first orders of business in our groups. In larger groups, the initial reporting of homework assignments can be quite time consuming. When this occurs, a number of smaller groups can be formed, each with a co-trainer. The co-trainer can then lead the subgroup in the reporting and sharing of homework assignments. Because we feel it is important for *each* member to share, discuss, and get some feedback on the behaviors occurring between the training sessions, we would recommend this subgroup procedure over skipping the reports entirely or dealing with just a few members each time.

During the early phases of training, some clients seem to be more prone to report their "failures" rather than their "successes." Because we try to focus more on the successes than the failures, and because dwelling on the failures tends to lower a person's self-confidence and self-esteem, we sometimes impose the rule that before individuals can tell us of their failures, they must first tell the group where they acted assertively during the past week. By doing this, we find that the group morale is higher, and that failures seem to lose much of their traumatic significance.

Occasionally, a person will come into group and state that he has not done a single assertive act during the past week. We tend to discount this statement and ask him to recall *any* assertive behaviors, no matter how small or insignificant the behaviors may seem. If this tack fails, we may resort to questions such as "Who got you dressed this morning?" "Did you talk to anyone during this past week without feeling extremely anxious or depressed?" or "Did anyone make you come to group today?" These may sound like ridiculous questions, but don't underestimate their value. Individuals with an extremely poor self-concept find it difficult to find *anything* positive in their actions. By focusing on some positives through these simple and basic questions, it is often possible to begin reversing the person's poor self-image. In some cases (especially with a hospitalized population), keeping records of even these basic behaviors may be very important to the treatment process.

Within-session assignments

We often do not wait until the next session before having the client do some "homework." On several occasions, after we have done some behavioral rehearsal in the group, we have asked the client to leave the therapy group and carry out a specific behavioral task. Upon completing the task, the individual is then to report back to the group. For example, when one male client was having difficulty giving direct eye contact to strangers (primarily women), we sent him out of the group for awhile *with* a co-therapist to practice giving eye contact to people he passed on the street. Here again the advantage of having two or more co-therapists present is evident.

On another occasion when we were conducting a group at a free clinic, we sent one of the members into the waiting room with instructions to begin a conversation with a stranger. More recently, we have begun sending two clients out together in order to complete specific assignments (e.g., the driver of the car asked for the battery water in his car to be checked, and the passenger asked for directions on how to reach a certain destination). One of the advantages of these "within-session assignments" is that they provide for more immediate success and feedback. In addition, they generate a tremendous amount of discussion and support from the other group members when the clients return.

It should also be noted that these between-session or within-session assignments are not limited to our private clients alone. At almost every assertion training workshop we have done for professionals, we ask them to carry out similar assignments. Before you give any homework assignment to one of your clients, we would recommend that you first carry out this task yourself. Some of the seemingly more simple assignments may generate a considerable amount of anxiety which you might become more aware of if you personally carry out the task. In addition, by doing the task yourself, you will be in a better position to role-play some of the responses that the client is likely to receive.

Sample homework assignments

With this as an introduction, we would now like to outline some of the homework assignments we have used in the past. This sample is by no means an exhaustive list of the situations you can utilize. Many such situations can be derived directly from one of the several assertion questionnaires that are now available (see Chapter 5). Other situations can be constantly derived from your own personal experiences or the experiences of others. As a case in point, Julio decided to go bowling one evening, and, after finishing one of his record games of 76, he went to get some coffee. As he was leaving the coffee shop with a cup in each hand, he approached the door which read "Pull to open." Not being agile enough to balance one cup on his head while he opened the door, he realized that he needed some help. He therefore turned to a stranger sitting nearby and asked if she would open the door for him. On the way out, Julio realized he had "invented" a new homework assignment. Consequently, during the next session, one of the members in the group who was experiencing difficulty in asking for things was instructed to go to the bowling alley and repeat the procedure Julio had gone through. (The individual was, however, given encouragement to bowl a better game.)

If you do assertion training, you should constantly be aware of potential homework assignments that come from your own personal experiences and that might be of value to your clients. Also, keep in mind that there is no predetermined order to these homework assignments. For each individual, you must first determine at what level he is able to successfully function. The assignments should then be designed in such a way that he gradually improves assertive skills with the likelihood of success being fairly high each step of the way. In fact, when a person is getting started in doing the homework assignments, we often begin with a behavior where the client has already demonstrated his success. This not only gives him an opportunity to receive some initial group support and practice in record keeping, but it also gives him increased confidence to try something a bit more difficult the next time. Remember, success breeds success!

1. To work on better eye contact, first have the person rate his SUDS while giving direct eye contact to someone on TV (e.g., a newscaster). Later have the person practice eye contact with people he passes on the street, at work, at a party, etc. As he becomes proficient in this, direct him to simultaneously smile and say "Hello."

2. Call the information operator and ask for a number and address. Ask the operator to repeat the information.

3. Go into a restaurant and order a salad with a certain kind of dressing on it. Then, as the waiter begins to walk away,

call him back and change the order (e.g., ask for a different dressing).

4. Go into a restaurant and order a hamburger (steak, etc.) done a certain way. *If* it is not done the way you ordered it, send it back to the kitchen and ask for it to be cooked the way you requested.

5. Pick out something in a restaurant that you enjoyed during the course of your meal (e.g., the service, the way the steak tasted, the atmosphere). Before leaving, find the manager/owner/chef and compliment him on this.

6. Go into a gas station and get less than a full tank of gas. Then find some service that the attendant has not completed and ask him to perform this service (e.g., wash the windows; check the oil, battery water, tires). If he states you need a new piece of equipment, thank him for pointing this out to you, but *do not* buy this item then and there.

7. Go into a restaurant and request a particular table.

8. Go into a market and buy one item. Then find a line where several people are waiting with large baskets filled with groceries. Go to the front of the line and ask if you can go through with your single item. (Do not try to cash a check if permission is given to go ahead.)

9. Buy an item in a retail store and return later to exchange it for something else. A more advanced assignment is to ask for a cash refund rather than credit or exchange.

10. Make, and then cancel, reservations at a fancy hotel or restaurant.

11. Pick out a stranger at a party, at work, or on a bus, and begin a conversation with this person.

12. Borrow an item from a neighbor.

13. When your spouse, friend, boss, or fellow employee does something you like, make a specific point of telling him what you liked.

14. Go into a gas station or stop someone on the street and ask for directions on how to get somewhere.

15. Go into a sporting goods store, plant store, hobby shop, art center, etc., and ask for some information on a product or activity in which you are interested.

16. Tell someone about a recent activity you completed and enjoyed (e.g., a skiing trip, a backpacking trip, a class you took).

17. Talk about a book or news item you recently read. (If the client has trouble with conversations and does not read very much, we might ask him to do some reading before attempting this assignment.)

18. Find some store where prices are not fixed, and then try to barter for the best price possible.

19. Find a place where the length of a conversation will be time limited and start a conversation (e.g., standing in line at a theater, market, post office; being in an elevator; getting a haircut; riding in a taxi).

20. During the course of a conversation with someone, keep track of the open-ended questions, free information, and self-disclosure statements that are being made by you and the other person.

21. Negotiate and try to get one of your needs met with a friend or spouse through the use of a contract.

22. Record the number of times you touch people during the course of a day. Then try to increase the number of touching responses during each succeeding day for a week.

23. Say something positive about yourself or give some free information to someone you know.

24. Take the day off and do something you enjoy, such as fishing, sailing, shopping, or reading a good book at a park.

25. As an ongoing assignment, we ask each group member to

try one new assertive behavior each week that he previously would not do or had avoided for some time.

Again, the above examples are provided as a representative sample of some of the homework assignments we have given during assertion training. However, the range of these tasks may be much broader and more complex, depending upon the individual needs and goals of the clients. At times, individuals will ask if they can set up their own homework assignment during the next week. If we feel this can be done without producing extremely high levels of anxiety, we will encourage the person to assume this responsibility.

As a final note, when we have presented the use of these homework assignments to other professionals, we occasionally receive criticism that these assignments take advantage of others (the service station attendant, the information operator, the person waiting in line in a market). We do not believe this is the case. In some cases this is part of the person's job (e.g., the service station attendant, the operator); and in other cases (e.g., the person waiting in line, the neighbor), the other individual does have the option to refuse the request. Also, whenever a request is made for some need to be satisfied, we emphasize that the client acknowledge and thank the other person if this request is met: Thanking the person is just as important as asking. It is also helpful to keep in mind that certain individuals who are often neglected by others (such as the elderly, the taxi driver, or the grocery store clerk) may enjoy talking with others; consequently, they may find conversations to be very pleasurable rather than an inconvenience.

After we have expressed the purpose and the value of the specific homework assignment, if the client or other trainer felt that this particular activity was still taking unfair advantage of another human being, we would back off of this assignment and try to find a homework assignment more agreeable to the client or trainer. Essentially, we do not believe that people should be asked to do something that they feel is morally wrong—regardless of whether or not this is couched in terms of a "useful therapeutic experience."

12 Evaluating progress

How do you go about evaluating any changes that might have occurred as a result of assertion training, and when are the benefits maximized to the point where the training can be terminated?

In our opinion, the outcome of assertion training is more difficult to evaluate than some of the other behavioral approaches. To begin with, the classification of "nonassertive" and "aggressive" behaviors covers a much broader area than other behaviorally defined problems such as "stuttering," "anorexia," "phobias," "impotency," and so forth. Consequently, within a group and within a single individual there may be a myriad of specific, well-defined goals. Because the specific goals and training needs can vary so much between different individuals, it is sometimes difficult to compare groups as being homogeneous or to consider two individuals as being matched controls.

Another factor to be considered is that assertion training involves a number of treatment approaches (behavioral rehearsal, modeling, desensitization, coaching, and positive reinforcement), each of which may be having a contributing effect to the overall process and outcome. As to what effect each of these components has and whether or not these effects differ with different presenting problems is a topic of current research.

Thirdly, and perhaps most important, much of the past writing in this area has come from the "private" sector of therapists and trainers where experimental design and statistical analysis is not weighted as heavily as just looking at some changes in behavior and self-report measures in a cursory manner. As a result, many of the beneficial

189

changes that are currently being reported have not been substantiated by statistical data to show the benefits of this training/treatment package in comparison to other approaches or the generalization and long-range effects that occur within the individual. However, this situation is rapidly changing as researchers in this area are now beginning to statistically evaluate some of their methods.

Evaluative measures

Although the above-mentioned factors may somewhat limit the conclusions we are able to draw at this time regarding the correlation between treatment and results, it is still possible to observe and evaluate certain client changes which appear to result from assertion training procedures. As with other behavioral approaches, these effects can be grouped into self-report, behavioral, and physiological changes. In this chapter we have presented some of the evaluative measures we are currently using to assess self-report, behavioral, and physiological changes. The final section outlines some criteria for deciding when the assertion training can be terminated.

Self-report measures

The self-report measures which we are most pleased with at this time come from our Assertive Data Collection Package. Three of these measures—the Assertion Training Diary, the Assertive Goal Scale, and the Homework Diary—contain information which is not only helpful during the training process, but which is also important to evaluating the final success or failure of treatment. Both the Assertion Training Diary and the Homework Diary call for the reporting of high and low anxiety levels (i.e., SUDS) when the client is engaged in assertive behaviors outside of the group. As these behaviors or very similar assertive behaviors are repeated several times throughout the training process, changes in anxiety levels can be statistically compared and evaluated for a given individual. A second comparison which can be made involves how successful the client views the completion of a given assertive act. A ten-point scale to access the success or failure of a given situation is included on the Home-work Diary sheet, and although this scale is not presented on the Assertion Training Diary or the Assertive Goal Scale, it can still be applied at a later date in order to collect more data for statistical evaluation purposes. Finally, if one is interested in measuring the frequency of recorded assertive responses as a result of assertion training, the Assertion Training Diary can be useful here. Our experience has been that as clients progress through the assertion training program, they begin to report increasingly more assertive incidents on their Assertion Training Diary. Although we have not yet used a control group to statistically compare the frequency of these reported events, the possibility certainly remains for one to do so.

Another measure of reported changes occurring outside of the group which can be used to evaluate progress is the paper-and-pencil questionnaire. Almost all of our clients are asked to complete at least one of these available questionnaires prior to beginning training and then at the conclusion of training (e.g., the questionnaires by Willoughby, 1934; Wolpe & Lang, 1964; Wolpe & Lazarus, 1966; Gambrill & Richey, 1972; Alberti & Emmons, 1974; our own questionnaire presented in Appendix B). We have some objections to evaluating these questionnaires in a statistical manner due to our concern over (1) the reliability and validity of these measures when each item on the questionnaire is not discussed individually and (2) the overall meaning of any total score (given that some "situational" nonassertive/aggressive individuals may score very low and still be in need of some assertion training). However, there is little doubt that self-report measures such as these will continue to be used in evaluating the outcome of assertion training; consequently, it would be most beneficial to develop paper-and-pencil self-report measures which would lend themselves to more accurate statistical evaluation.

With respect to self-report changes occurring within the group, we are constantly asking individuals how relaxed or tense they are feeling in terms of their SUDS throughout the training process. This self-report measure not only dictates what we present at any given time, but also at what pace we proceed. Without this self-report measure, we think our assertion training procedures would be much less effective. We know that the individual's reported SUDS decreases during the sessions because without this decrease we would not move on to any new material. However, what is needed now is to look at these changes from a statistical standpoint.

Behavioral changes

With respect to behavioral changes that occur within the group setting, there are a number of specific behaviors related to assertion that one may wish to record and statistically evaluate. Some of the "simpler" behaviors to record and score include the number of words, self-disclosures, and items of free information emitted during the training session; the frequency of touching responses; and voice level. Some of the more "complex" behaviors include the ability to role-play, coach, and interact with others during the group session or the types of behavioral responses, both verbal and nonverbal, given to a videotaped or filmed dramatization. We have not yet evaluated these behaviors in a statistical manner, but there is no reason why behavioral observation sheets cannot be devised, baseline data collected, and specific behaviors tabulated and statistically evaluated by the therapist or by an impartial observer.

In one attempt to evaluate behavioral changes occurring outside of the group, McFall & Lillesand (1971) had a confederate of the therapist call the client and try to persuade the individual to do something such as buy a magazine or volunteer time. Although there may be some concerns in using this approach (e.g., dependent measures used, new ethical standards related to research), it does represent another attempt to evaluate change across a different behavioral dimension.

Physiological changes

With respect to physiological changes occurring as a result of assertion training, very little data has been reported in the literature. In fact, only one assertion training study reports the use of a physiological dependent variable—pulse rate—and in this study the results were not significant (McFall & Marston, 1970). It is our belief, however, that increasingly more data will be published in this area within the near future.

It does not appear to be a major step in moving from the present self-report measure of SUDS to the monitoring of the individual's physiological state through the use of biofeedback equipment. Along these lines, we have already employed the use of a small heart-rate monitor in order to provide feedback to some of our clients during relaxation training, and, with some newer equipment, we plan to monitor some of their physiological responses as they carry out the various functions of behavioral rehearsal and coaching. As a further extension of this idea, it seems quite reasonable with some of the more sophisticated and portable biofeedback equipment that an individual could monitor and keep records of his own physiological responses (e.g., heart rate, galvanic skin response, temperature change) as he carries out various assertive tasks in the natural environment. There is no doubt that our current technology is advanced enough to evaluate physioloical changes occurring in assertion training in a more sophisticated manner than has been done in the past. However, as with most research endeavors, this requires a considerable amount of expense and time in terms of equipment and people.

Termination

The question of termination would seem to be an easy issue to deal with in a time-limited group where the number of sessions has been specified at the beginning of the group. If, by the last session, the individual has been able to achieve some of his goals on the Assertive Goal Scale at a satisfactory level, if the individual has shown an increasingly greater ability to respond more assertively in the groups via behavioral rehearsal, if the individual is reporting less SUDS with each session and this seems to be corroborated by observation and the ADCP materials, then there may be no serious problem in termination. Some gains have been made and the individual is moving in a direction that he will hopefully be able to sustain and enhance even further as time goes on. However, what happens if, by the end of the last session, the individual has shown little or no improvement, or, due to some unforeseen negative consequence which occurred to the individual when he tried to act assertively, he has shown some regression? We know that individuals do not all progress at the same rate, and we know there are occasionally some setbacks that require additional time to be worked out.

In our own groups, if we and the client both feel that the goals of training have not yet been achieved when the group as a whole is ready to be closed (and that assertion training is still a viable means of reaching these goals), we will make arrangements for the client to be "recycled" into another group or we will see the client on an individual basis until another group is started. In a research study where specific variables are being investigated, this may be difficult to arrange. However, it is our belief that once an individual has sought some help in this area (which may have been very anxiety-provoking in the first place), he should be given every opportunity to achieve at least *some success* and a resolution to some of the presenting problems—even if this involves working with the individual after the research is completed, or, in a private practice, after the client's funds have run out.

Finally, some follow-up is also important after the individual has stopped being seen on a regular basis. Some of this follow-up can be readily accomplished by having the individual return to another group as a visitor, contacting the person by telephone, or sending the individual a questionnaire to be filled out and returned. Based upon the research findings (see Chapter 14), there is little doubt that assertion training is useful in changing some specific behaviors and enhancing a person's self-concept over a short period of time. However, it is now important to verify that these changes are longlasting and to what extent this training generalizes to similar and other areas of functioning in the person's life.

13 Conclusion

From its origin as a procedure for freeing individuals of their inhibitory behaviors (Salter, 1949) and reducing anxiety (Wolpe, 1958), assertion training has evolved into a rather elaborate set of procedures aimed at teaching social skills and enhancing self-respect. As such, it has been used with clients in all walks of life—private clients, hospitalized patients, college students, couples, children, adolescents, businessmen—in addressing a wide variety of interpersonal problems. For those of you who are specifically interested in training others, we have listed fifty points in the section below which we believe represent some of the more important aspects of assertion training. Hopefully, these points will serve as a useful checklist which you can refer to and use in your ongoing assertive teaching and behaviors.

1. Before teaching assertion training to others, be assertive yourself! This means that you should be able to carry out most, if not all, of the trainer's functions described in this book without experiencing high amounts of anxiety and that your responses on the several assessment questionnaires would be highly assertive. In addition, you or your co-therapist should have some reading background and experience in learning theory, and each of you should have some firsthand exposure to assertion training before you start an assertion group of your own (e.g., taking a class on assertion training, being a co-therapist in another assertion group).

2. Group assertion training offers several advantages not found in individual assertion training; therefore, consider utilizing this treatment modality whenever possible.

3. Whenever possible, use two or more therapists when conducting an assertion training group. At least one of these co-therapists should be of the opposite sex in order to promote better identification and behavioral rehearsal experiences as well as better understanding. Other minority or ethnic representation may also be advantageous if the population of the group suggests this.

4. Choose a co-therapist you enjoy working with as a friend as well as a fellow professional.

5. Talk to your co-therapist about what you see and believe is going on both within and outside of the group setting. Do not be afraid to disagree with your co-therapist in front of the group—this is one excellent way to model resolving differences.

6. Be ready to come to the aid of your co-therapist if he gets stuck. Your co-therapist will be a great help to you—appreciate him/her.

7. Remember that as one of the leaders of the group, you are an important model for your clients. Utilize this modeling potential whenever possible.

8. If treatment fails, you are partially responsible—remember this.

9. In utilizing questionnaires to evaluate the client's non-assertive/aggressive behaviors, go over the questionnaire items in detail with the client.

10. Do not be afraid of putting aggressive and nonassertive individuals in the same group—they will learn from one another.

11. Before you request an individual to do something (e.g., behavioral rehearsal, coach someone else, homework assignment), tell him the reason for making this request, your goals, and what he might expect to experience in carrying out this request. This builds trust and helps to maintain low anxiety levels.

12. Emphasize that assertion is a group of skills that can be

learned to a greater or lesser degree and which can enhance self-respect and dignity.

13. Have clients set some specific goals as to what they would like to see accomplished as a result of assertion training. Discuss and, if necessary, revise these goals periodically.

14. Try to insure success whenever possible. This means avoiding steps and homework assignments that are too large for the client to handle successfully. This also involves the use of shaping and behavioral hierarchies throughout the therapy process. Remember, start with something simple where the probability of success is very high and the anxiety is very low.

15. Utilize SUDS to monitor the clients' anxiety levels as they engage in the various assertive behaviors.

16. Avoid confrontation and encounter experiences. In most cases, assertion training follows a desensitization model (Wolpe 1958, 1969) and not an implosion model (Stampfl & Levis, 1967).

17. Unless you are purposely trying to implode the client (Stampfl & Levis, 1967), keep the anxiety as low as possible and gradually work up to more stressful situations.

18. Support and reinforce clients' *efforts* as well as their successes—very, very frequently.

19. Discuss the potential dangers of the client being assertive with other individuals who wish to maintain a one-upmanship position. Also keep in mind that, under some circumstances, a client may be willing to terminate a relationship such as a marriage or job in order to acquire or maintain his dignity and self-respect.

20. Attempt to avoid severe punitive consequences whenever possible. Teach the client how to discriminate when being assertive might lead to punitive consequences that the *client believes* outweigh the merits of acting assertively at that particular time. A person can be basically assertive and still choose not to act assertively in specific instances.

21. A person can act assertively and still not get his needs met on every occasion. One of the goals of assertion is to increase the probability that these needs will be met—it does not assume, however, that the needs will be satisfied all of the time. Even if the individual does not get his needs met, he can still be made to feel good for asking.

22. In making a request, teach the client how to ask for something a second time before giving up.

23. Be prepared for client failures, and have procedures ready that will help to eliminate similar failures in the future. Also, try to find some positives even if the client fails.

24. Be prepared for the client over-utilizing his assertive skills when these skills are first being learned (especially the defensive techniques), and, where appropriate, share this knowledge with the client.

25. Assertion training is an active process—be an active therapist and encourage your clients to take an active role in the group.

26. Emphasize and practice behavioral rehearsal, modeling, coaching, and positive reinforcement as much as possible during the sessions.

27. Reinforce good actors and actresses in the group for their role-playing abilities.

28. When the trainer acts as a coach in behavioral rehearsal, fade the coaching gradually and allow the client to assume more and more responsibility for the interaction.

29. As the clients become familiar with the behavioral rehearsal procedure, give them the opportunity to coach other clients in being more assertive.

30. Give frequent homework assignments that are geared to the appropriate ability level and anxiety level of the client.

31. Have the clients keep a weekly record of their homework assignments that are carried out as well as a record of

those situations where they acted in an assertive, non-assertive, or aggressive manner. The record sheet should also contain the client's anxiety level (i.e., SUDS) that occurred when the situation took place.

32. Homework assignments should be ultimately related to the individual's goals for seeking assistance in the first place.

33. Emphasize the positive assertive skills that foster closer relationships (e.g., positive feedback, contracting) as well as the assertive skills that protect the individual from being victimized by others.

34. Before a client utilizes any of the protective techniques, he should first try to convey his feelings through a clear, honest communication. Only if this communication is ignored should the person then consider the use of a protective technique.

35. Teach negotiation and contracting that does not sacrifice the dignity and self-respect of the client *or* the other person.

36. Discourage excessive apologies and similar behaviors that tend to tear down a person's positive self-image and that tend to inhibit open communication.

37. Remember the nonassertive "myths"—all of these are dangerous traps to enhanced self-respect.

38. Teach your clients how to give and how to accept compliments graciously. Both of these functions are important to a better self-concept.

39. Do not be afraid to use touch (and teach touching) as a distraction to anxiety and as an important source of strong positive reinforcement.

40. Do not be afraid to try something new—be creative and flexible.

41. Whenever possible, work with significant others (e.g., parents, spouse, boss, teacher) in order to teach all parties

concerned a more equitable way of relating to one another.

42. The nonverbal behaviors that a person emits may be as important as the verbal message. As such, both dimensions are important in assertion training.

43. Have clients overlearn assertive skills so that they will be better prepared to handle future situations that are potentially more stressful than the ones they describe during the group.

44. Frequently bring visitors into the group, and make them an active part of the group process.

45. If available, try to utilize equipment such as audio tape recorders, videotape, films, and the like in order to enhance the learning process.

46. Assertion training can be an enjoyable process for the trainers as well as the clients. Do not be afraid to use humor in your groups. Remember, humor can be a counter-conditioning agent to anxiety (relaxation, thinking, and distraction also serve this purpose).

47. Collect data which can be used to provide feedback to the client and which can be helpful to others doing research in this area.

48. Provide for follow-up and support after the training has terminated.

49. Each individual that you see and work with is a unique and different human being. His needs may be different, his treatment goals may be different, and the assertive skills he feels most comfortable in using may be different. Be willing to utilize your individual skills and expertise as a therapist to fit the individual needs of your client. Also, do not ask your client to carry out any behaviors that he feels are ethically or morally wrong.

50. Enjoy yourself. Assertion training can be a valuable and stimulating experience for you as well as your clients.

Open, honest communication. Learning how to relax and reduce anxiety. Getting more of your needs met. Learning social skills that form closer interpersonal relationships. Being able to verbally and nonverbally communicate your positive and negative feelings, thoughts, and emotions without experiencing undue amounts of anxiety or guilt and without violating the dignity of others. Taking responsibility for what happens to you in life. Making more decisions and free choices. Being a friend to yourself and maintaining your own dignity and self-respect. Recognizing that you have certain rights and value system that need not be sacrificed. Being able to protect yourself from being victimized and taken advantage of by others. Discriminating as to when assertive behaviors may lead to negative as well as positive consequences.

Essentially this is what we believe assertion training is all about. It is not aggression training whereby you transgress upon the rights and dignity of another person. It is not a means of manipulating or deceiving others in order to just get ahead. On the contrary, assertion training, as we see it, rests upon a foundation of respect—respect for yourself, respect for others, and respect for your own value system from others.

It is our opinion that individuals who are able to openly and honestly communicate their wants, wishes, needs, value systems, opinions, and concerns without violating the rights of others are in a much better position to feel better about themselves and obtain more of what they are asking for in life. This does not assume that they will act assertively one hundred percent of the time or that they will be successful each and every time they are assertive. However, there is a basic assumption that more needs will be satisfied by being assertive than by remaining passively quiet or being overtly aggressive. What we have presented in the previous chapters is one way of assisting individuals to achieve more of their psychological and material goals. Certainly it is not the only approach of value, nor is it necessarily the best approach for everyone to teach. Therapists teaching assertive skills in a systematic manner as we have presented here should recognize that they assume a great deal of responsibility for the welfare of their clients as well as for the welfare of those with whom the client interacts. For it is the therapist who models, coaches, supports, and often directs the assertive efforts of the individual. As such, it is extremely important that the therapist make every effort to insure that these assertive procedures are used in a manner that will not be punitive to the client or to others in the client's environment.

Also, it was not our intent that this book be used as a perfect template to be followed by others without any variations. In many ways what we do and what we have presented here is uniquely us. In reading this book—whether you are a trainer or a client—we hope that you will now be in a better place to discover what is *assertively and uniquely you.*

14 Review of the literature

Compared to other behavioral procedures, assertion training has received relatively little attention in the literature. In his 1950-1969 *Behavior Therapy Bibliography*, containing close to nine hundred references, Morrow (1971) cited only 53 references in the area of assertion training. However, this situation has changed dramatically over the past few years. In a 1974 critical review paper, Jacobs cited 31 references on assertion training written *after* 1969. Yet, both of these totals are misleading in that many of the component procedures that make up what has come to be known as "assertion training" have been researched and indexed separately under titles such as modeling, behavioral rehearsal, systematic desensitization, shaping, and positive reinforcement. Consequently, this is not a totally new procedure, but is rather a relatively recent "package of procedures" known as *assertion training.*

Perhaps the best place to begin is with Salter's (1949) book entitled *Conditioned Reflex Therapy.* In this book Salter described his prescribed response styles in terms of "feeling talk" (i.e., saying what you feel); "facial talk" (i.e., the corresponding nonverbal expression of feelings); the ability to make "contradict and attack" statements when disagreeing with someone; the frequent use of "I" statements; the ability to accept praise and compliments; the ability to praise oneself; and the ability to live for the present and be spontaneous. Salter called these six rules the *excitatory reflexes,* and his book contains 57 case studies where these "excitatory reflexes" were used in the treatment of a wide variety of symptoms such as claustrophobia, shyness, low self-sufficiency, depression, sexual problems, psychosomatic problems, stuttering, and alcohol addiction. Although these excitatory reflexes have been equated with assertive behaviors, Salter (1974) has recently stated that excitation is a more global theory and that "assertion training is merely a wart on the pickle of excitation." Nevertheless, many of the procedures currently found in the assertion training literature can be found in Salter's earlier 1949 publication. Consequently, it is an excellent text for both the therapist and client who are interested in teaching or acquiring assertive skills (Wolpe & Lazarus, 1966; Lesser, 1967; and Alberti & Emmons, 1970 indicated that they assigned this book to their clients as a reading assignment).

Joseph Wolpe has also made some major contributions to the area of assertion training. In a number of his writings, Wolpe (1958, 1969, 1970) presented assertion training as one of the major procedures by which an individual can reciprocally inhibit and, consequently, eliminate anxiety. Whereas Salter (1949) applied his "excitatory reflexes" almost universally to the patients he described, Wolpe (1958) found these procedures (which he preferred to label as "assertive" rather than "excitatory") of value only for overcoming unadaptive anxiety that appears in the course of interpersonal relationships. Wolpe (1969) stated that assertion training is not appropriate in cases where noninterpersonal anxiety exists (e.g., fear of heights, fear of animals, fear of darkness) or in some circumscribed social situations where anxiety is evoked by the mere presence of a particular individual. In these latter cases, Wolpe (1958, 1969) prefers the utilization of systematic desensitization.

In addition to Salter's (1949) *response inhibition* theory for explaining the presence of inappropriate behaviors (consequently, the need for "excitation") and Wolpe's (1958) *anxiety and avoidance* hypothesis for the occurrence of nonassertive behaviors, there is another explanation. This third explanation assumes that the appropriate assertive behaviors are not in the individual's behavioral repertoire from the beginning. This third conceptual model is briefly discussed in the Wolpe & Lazarus (1966) book entitled *Behavior Therapy Techniques* and has also been presented by Laws & Serber

(1971) and by Hersen, Eisler & Miller (1973). In the Wolpe & Lazarus (1966) book, the authors not only indicated that individuals have certain basic assertive "rights" which they are entitled to exercise, but that anxiety, somatic symptoms, and pathological changes in predisposed organs can result if these "rights" are not acted upon. Therefore, anxiety may be only one of several negative consequences resulting from non-assertion or aggression. The authors also described in some detail many of the treatment variables currently found in assertion training (e.g., the hierarchical presentation of stimulus situations; the use of shaping techniques, behavioral rehearsal, modeling, and homework assignments; the value of audio feedback to the client). This, too, is a useful reference source for those interested in carrying out assertion training procedures with others.

Between 1966 and 1970, the number of articles on assertion training and assertion-related procedures began to increase dramatically. In 1966, Wolpe co-authored two books (Wolpe & Lazarus, 1966; Wolpe, Salter & Reyna, 1966), both of which contained material on assertion training. In the same year, Lazarus (1966) reported on a study comparing behavioral rehearsal with giving direct advice and nondirective, reflection-interpretation therapy in the management of private clients with interpersonal problems. His results (based on his clinical judgment of *in vivo* behavioral changes) indicated that behavioral rehearsal was effective in 92% of the cases, direct advice was effective in 44% of the cases, and nondirective therapy was effective in 32% of the cases. A later article by Lazarus (1968) is one of the first descriptions of how to conduct assertion training in groups. In this article he described some of the conditions necessary for conducting such a group as well as many of the specific procedures used. For those individuals interested in conducting various types of behavior therapy in groups, the Lazarus article can be very useful.

In 1968, Wagner reported that hospitalized patients who were taught to express anger in a role-playing situation, and who were positively reinforced for doing so, showed a significantly greater ability in their anger expressiveness compared to individuals who were negatively reinforced for the expression of anger and compared to a control group. In a different hospital study, Wilson & Smith (1968) reported on the successful four-session treatment of a hospitalized patient with multiple problems using a modified desensitization procedure, assertion training, and family therapy. One year later, Piaget & Lazarus (1969) described the combination of behavioral rehearsal and systematic desensitization (which they called "rehearsal desensitization") in treating several clinical cases. That same year, Krumboltz & Thoresen (1969) edited a book of readings in behavioral counseling which contained four different reports (by Geisinger, Hosford, Newman, and Vorenhorst) of therapy where assertion training and/or assertion-related procedures were successfully employed.

Beginning in 1970, the interest and research in assertion training began to proliferate. In 1970, Alberti and Emmons published a short book entitled *Your Perfect Right: A Guide to Assertive Behavior* which is, perhaps, one of the best reference books on assertion training since Salter's 1949 text (the Alberti & Emmons book was revised in 1974). The book does not cite any hard research data by the authors (an annotated bibliography on some research data is presented in the second edition); however, it does give several situations where assertive behaviors may be appropriate and describes how these behaviors are closely related to humanistic philosophy.

In changing the label of "patient" to "trainee" and that of the "therapist" to "facilitator," Alberti & Emmons (1970) drew attention to the teacher-student relationship that exists in assertion training—Fensterheim (1972) has also pointed this out—and to the fact that many of the groups where assertion principles have been presented do not fall under the traditional classification of a "patient" group. Lazarus (1968) indicated that the therapist may be more of a participant-observer than a therapist or instructor in that each client is a therapeutic agent for other clients in the assertion group.

Alberti & Emmons (1970, 1974) also discussed assertion training done in groups (previously discussed by Lazarus in

206

1968) which has increasingly become the treatment of choice in recent years (Hedquist & Weinhold, 1970; Fensterheim, 1972; Booraem & Flowers, 1972; Shoemaker & Paulson, 1973; Cotler, 1973, 1975; Bloomfield, 1973; Flowers & Guerra, 1974). Alberti and Emmons also described in some detail the differentiation between the "generalized" and the "situational" nonassertive/aggressive individual.

The same year that the Alberti and Emmons book was first published, McFall & Marston (1970) published a study dealing with a semi-automated, standardized form of behavioral rehearsal (with and without feedback) for male and female nonassertive college students. Using a variety of measures, their results indicated that the combined behavioral rehearsal groups did better than two control groups.

A later study with college students by McFall & Lillesand (1971) tested the effectiveness of behavioral rehearsal with modeling and coaching. Subjects in an "overt" group practiced their assertive responses aloud and heard a recorded replay of their behavior. A "covert" behavioral rehearsal group also received modeling and coaching, but the subjects spent time reflecting on their responses and did not hear a recorded replay of their assertive behavior. Compared to the control group, both treatment groups showed greater improvement on various measures with respect to refusing unreasonable requests, and on some measures the "covert" group was superior to the "overt" behavioral rehearsal group. Another important finding from this study was that although the learning had generalized to other untrained refusal situations it did not generalize to other forms of assertive behaviors. Consequently, it may be important and necessary for the individual to have some training experience with each of the situations he is experiencing difficulty with in the outside world.

In a third and more complex study using college students, McFall & Twentyman (1973) attempted to evaluate the relative contribution that rehearsal, modeling, and coaching made to the assertion process. Their results indicated that both the rehearsal and the coaching components contribute an independent and additive effect to the assertion training process. Flowers & Guerra (1974) also found that coaching was an important variable in their study using probation officers as subjects.

Other studies, using nonassertive college students as subjects, where the variables of modeling, rehearsal, and/or coaching were either evaluated and/or used as an integral part of the procedure include Hedquist & Weinhold (1970), Friedman (1971), Rathus (1972), and Young, Rimm & Kennedy (1973). In each of these studies, the variables of modeling, rehearsal, coaching, or combinations of these procedures proved superior to the various control groups that were used for comparison. In a later study by Rathus (1973b), nonassertive women met for seven sessions, during which time the experimental subjects viewed videotapes, practiced assertive behaviors, and kept track of their assertive behaviors during the week. Compared to a placebo treatment group and a no treatment group, the women's group receiving assertion training reported significantly more assertive behaviors on the Rathus Assertiveness Schedule (Rathus, 1973a) and on the taped interviews.

In addition to the studies published with college students as the subject population, a number of other studies has more recently appeared with hospitalized patients as the treatment population. Weinman et al. (1972) were able to obtain significant behavioral and self-report changes in assertiveness, interaction, and reduced anxiety level over a three-month period with a group of males labeled as chronic schizophrenics. Bach, Lowry & Maylan (1972) also obtained assertive behavioral changes with a group of male and female in-patients who practiced refusing unreasonable requests. Booraem & Flowers (1972), in working with male psychotic patients, obtained significant improvements in a self-report measure and a personal space measure following assertion training. Other assertion studies using hospitalized patients as subjects include Lomont et al. (1969), Eisler, Miller & Hersen (1973), Hersen et al. (1973), and Longin & Rooney (1973).

With respect to out-patient populations, assertion training has been used by itself or in conjunction with other behavioral procedures in both individual and group settings in order to treat a wide variety of presenting problems (Salter, 1949; Wolpe, 1958, 1969, 1970, 1973; Stevenson & Wolpe, 1960; Wolpe & Lazarus, 1966; Lazarus, 1966, 1968, 1971; Neuman, 1969; Alberti & Emmons, 1970, 1974; Fensterheim, 1972; Eisler & Hersen, 1972; Edwards, 1972; Shoemaker & Paulson, 1973; Bloomfield, 1973; Guerra & Horsky, 1973; Cotler, 1973). Whereas many of the earlier studies employed individualized therapy, assertion training in a group setting has become increasingly more popular (Lazarus, 1968; Fensterheim, 1972; Alberti & Emmons, 1974; Shoemaker & Paulson, 1973; Jakubowski-Spector, 1973; Guerra & Horsky, 1973; Cotler, 1975). With respect to this recent group trend, Lazarus (1968), Fensterheim (1972), and Alberti & Emmons (1974) are particularly illustrative of the procedures employed.

The increasing popularity of assertion training can be attested to by the number of new books currently being published in this area. *The Assertive Woman* (Phelps & Austin, 1975); *Stand Up, Speak Out, Talk Back* (Alberti & Emmons, 1975); *Don't Say Yes When You Want To Say No* (Fensterheim & Baer, 1975); and *I Can If I Want To* (Lazarus & Fay, 1975) are excellent additions to the area of assertion training, and they can be extremely helpful to both professional and nonprofessional audiences.

Appendix A
Client Introduction Sheet

What is assertion?

Assertion is the *learned* ability to express your feelings and preferences, when you feel them, without upsetting others. It is the ability to exercise one's own rights without infringing upon the rights of others.

What is assertion training?

Assertion training involves acquiring skills in giving and receiving compliments *easily*; beginning, maintaining, and ending conversations with others *as we choose*; being able to express how we are feeling *without discomfort*; and how to avoid being taken advantage of by others. In general, we acquire more choice and control over our lives and respect ourselves more for these self-directed changes.

We meet in small groups of six to eight people and actually practice expressing our feelings and preferences with those who have the same goals as ourselves. The skills are practiced and acquired on a level that is comfortable for the individual participant.

What is nonassertion?

Nonassertion is represented by two extremes of learned behavior: either holding back one's feelings and denying their expression, or achieving one's goals aggressively at the expense of others. Sometimes a person can be nonassertive in a number of instances until his feelings build to a point where they are explosively (aggressively) delivered. Thus, a person's behavior can be like a pendulum, it can swing between passivity and aggression.

211

Nonassertive behavior is learned.

Being nonassertive is the learned practice of holding back one's feelings and denying their expression. We often experience our nonassertiveness *after* some "incident" when we might say to ourselves:

"I can never say no. I always seem to let others take advantage of me."

"I just didn't know how to react to his/her compliment."

We learn from the time we are very young *not* to express our feelings. We are taught to hold them inside by many of society's rules:

"Don't talk back to your elders."

"Your teacher knows best."

Soon we start to believe:

"If I say what I feel, I will hurt others and feel guilty."

Assertive behavior can be learned.

Just as nonassertive behavior is learned, it can be replaced by newly acquired assertive skills.

Reprinted with permission from W. Grimes, M. Moser & C. Smith. *Assertion training.* La Mesa, CA: Grossmont Psychological Associates, 1975.

Appendix B
Assertive Data Collection
Package Recording Forms

The Assertive Data Collection Package consists of self-report, paper-and-pencil measures which are used in the initial assessment phase of treatment to determine the extent of the individual's assertive difficulties, and which are also used throughout the treatment period to monitor progress. These measures include:

Assertiveness Inventory
Subjective Units of Discomfort (SUDS) Diary
Assertion Training Diary
Assertive Goal Scale
Homework Diary

Assertiveness Inventory

The following questions will be helpful in assessing your assertiveness. Be honest in your responses and draw a circle around the number that describes you best. Key: 0 means *no* or *never*; 1 means *somewhat* or *sometimes*; 2 means *average*; 3 means *usually* or *a good deal*; and 4 means *practically always* or *entirely*.

1. When you feel a person is being highly unfair to you, do you call it to his or her attention?   0 1 2 3 4

2. Do you find it difficult to make decisions?   0 1 2 3 4

3. Can you be openly critical of others' ideas, opinions, behavior?   0 1 2 3 4

4. Do you speak out in protest when someone takes your place in a line?   0 1 2 3 4

5. Do you often avoid people or situations for fear of embarrassment?   0 1 2 3 4

6. Do you usually have confidence in your own judgment?   0 1 2 3 4

7. Do you insist that your spouse or roommate take on a fair share of household chores?   0 1 2 3 4

8. Are you prone to "fly off the handle"?   0 1 2 3 4

9. When a salesperson makes an effort to sell you something, do you find it hard to say "No" even though the merchandise is not really what you want?   0 1 2 3 4

10. When a latecomer is waited on before you are, do you call attention to the situation?   0 1 2 3 4

11. Are you reluctant to speak up in a discussion or debate?   0 1 2 3 4

12. If a person has borrowed money (or a book, garment, or thing of value) and is overdue in returning it, do you mention it?   0 1 2 3 4

13. Do you continue to pursue an argument after the other person has had enough?   0 1 2 3 4

14. Do you generally express what you feel?   0 1 2 3 4

15. Are you disturbed if someone watches you work?   0 1 2 3 4

16. If someone keeps kicking or bumping your chair in a movie or a lecture, do you ask the person to stop?   0 1 2 3 4

17. Do you find it difficult to keep eye contact when talking to another person?   0 1 2 3 4

18. In a good restaurant, when your meal is improperly prepared or served, do you ask the waiter/waitress to correct the situation?   0 1 2 3 4

19. When you discover merchandise is faulty, do you return it for an adjustment?   0 1 2 3 4

20. Do you show anger by name calling or obscenities?   0 1 2 3 4

21. Do you try to be a wallflower or a piece of furniture in social situations?   0 1 2 3 4

22. Do you insist that your landlord (mechanic, repairman, etc.) make repairs, adjustments or replacements which are his responsibility?   0 1 2 3 4

23. Do you often step in and make decisions for others?   0 1 2 3 4

24. Are you able to openly express love and affection?   0 1 2 3 4

25. Are you able to ask your friends for small favors or help?   0 1 2 3 4

26. Do you think you always have the right answer?   0 1 2 3 4

27. When you differ with a person you respect, are you able to speak up for your own viewpoint?   0 1 2 3 4

28. Are you able to refuse requests made by a friend if you do not wish to do what the person is asking?   0 1 2 3 4

29. Do you have difficulty complimenting or praising others?   0 1 2 3 4

30. If you are disturbed by someone smoking near you, can you say so?   0 1 2 3 4

31. Do you shout or use bullying tactics to get others to do as you wish?   0 1 2 3 4

32. Do you finish other people's sentences for them?   0 1 2 3 4

33. Do you get into physical fights with others?   0 1 2 3 4

34. At meals, do you control and dominate the conversation?   0 1 2 3 4

35. When you meet a stranger, are you the first to introduce yourself and begin a conversation?   0 1 2 3 4

36. Do you compliment or praise others when they do something you like or appreciate?   0 1 2 3 4

37. Do you say "I am sorry" a good deal of the time when you do not really mean it?   0 1 2 3 4

38. Can you tell someone directly that you do not like what he/she is doing?   0 1 2 3 4

39. Do you usually try to avoid "bossy" people?   0 1 2 3 4

40. Do you usually keep your opinions to yourself?   0 1 2 3 4

41. When you receive a compliment, do you
tend to discount it in your own mind?   0 1 2 3 4

42. If a person is criticizing you unjustly, can
you defend yourself verbally rather than
hitting the person or walking away angry
and upset?   0 1 2 3 4

43. Can you tell things about yourself that
you like in front of others?   0 1 2 3 4

Adapted with permission from R. E. Alberti & M. L. Emmons. *Your perfect right.* San Luis Obispo, CA: Impact, 1974.

218

Subjective Units of Discomfort (SUDS) Diary

Name _____

Date	SUDS	Describe situation	Describe anxiety/relaxation responses
	0-9		
	10-19		
	20-29		
	30-39		
	40-49		
	50-59		
	60-69		
	70-79		
	80-89		
	90-100		

Assertion Training Diary

Name _____

Date	Assertion-related situation	SUDS High-Low	A) What happened? and B) How did you feel?	Future goals related to this situation

Assertive Goal Scale

Name _____ Date _____

	Goal No. 1	Goal No. 2	Goal No. 3	Goal No. 4
Describe your long-range goal.				
Where would you like your SUDS level to be when you achieve this goal?				
How long do you think it will take to achieve this long-range goal?				
Describe at least one short-range goal that will help you achieve your long-range goal.				

	Goal No. 1	Goal No. 2	Goal No. 3	Goal No. 4
Where would you like your SUDS level to be when you achieve this short-range goal?				
How long do you think it will take to achieve this short-range goal?				
What do you anticipate your SUDS will be when you first assert in this short-range situation?				
What is the worst possible outcome of your anxiety in this long-range goal?				
Number in order how important this long-range goal is in relation to the others you have listed.				

221

Homework Diary

Name _____

Date	Homework assignment	SUDS High-Low	What did you do?	Evaluate your success in completing assignment 0 (none) 5 (moderate) 10 (completely successful)	Future goals

References

Alberti, R. E. & Emmons, M. L. *Your perfect right: A guide to assertive behavior.* San Luis Obispo, CA: Impact, 1970.

Alberti, R. E. & Emmons, M. L. *Your perfect right* (2nd ed.). San Luis Obispo, CA: Impact, 1974.

Alberti, R. E. & Emmons, M. L. *Stand up, speak out, talk back.* New York: Pocket Books, 1975.

Bach, G. R. & Wyden, P. *The intimate enemy.* New York: William Morrow & Co., Inc., 1968.

Bach, R. C., Lowry, D. & Maylan, J. J. Training state hospital patients to be appropriately assertive. *Proceedings of the American Psychological Association,* 1972.

Bandura, A. *Principles of behavior modification.* New York: Holt, Rinehart and Winston, Inc., 1969.

Bates, H. D. & Zimmerman, S. F. Toward the development of a screening scale for assertive training. *Psychological Reports,* 1971, *28,* 99-107.

Bernstein, D. A. & Borkovec, T. D. *Progressive relaxation training: A manual for the helping professions.* Champaign, IL: Research Press Co., 1973.

Bloomfield, H. H. Assertive training in an outpatient group of chronic schizophrenics: A preliminary report. *Behavior Therapy,* 1973, *4,* 277-281.

Booraem, C. D. & Flowers, J. V. Reduction of anxiety and personal space as a function of assertion training with severely disturbed neuropsychiatric inpatients. *Psychological Reports,* 1972, *30,* 923-929.

Buss, A. H. *Psychopathology.* New York: John Wiley & Sons, Inc., 1966.

Cotler, S. B. How to train others to do assertion training: A didactic group model. Paper presented at Western Psychological Association, Anaheim, CA, April, 1973.

Cotler, S. B. Assertion training: A road leading where? *The Counseling Psychologist,* 1975, *5,* 20-29.

Cotler, S. B. & Guerra, J. J. *Relaxation training.* Sherman Oaks, CA: New Views Unlimited, 1975. (Audio cassette tape)

DeRisi, W. J. & Butz, G. *Writing behavioral contracts: A case simulation practice manual.* Champaign, IL: Research Press Co., 1975.

Edwards, N. B. Case conference: Assertive training in a case of homosexual pedophilia. *Journal of Behavior Therapy and Experimental Psychiatry,* 1972, *3,* 55-63.

Eisler, R. M. & Hersen, M. Some considerations in the measurement and modification of marital interaction. Paper presented at the Association for Advancement of Behavior Therapy, New York, 1972.

Eisler, R. M., Miller, P. M. & Hersen, M. Components of assertive behavior. *Journal of Clinical Psychology,* 1973, *3,* 295-299.

Eisler, R. M., Miller, P. M., Hersen, M. & Alford, H. Effects of assertion training on marital interaction. *Archives of General Psychiatry,* 1974, *30,* 643-649.

Fensterheim, H. Behavior therapy: Assertive training in groups. In C. J. Sager & H. Kaplan (Eds.), *Progress in group and family therapy.* New York: Brunner/Mazel, Inc., 1972.

Fensterheim, H. & Baer, J. *Don't say yes when you want to say no.* New York: David McKay Co., 1975.

Flowers, J. V. & Guerra, J. J. The use of client-coaching in assertion training with large groups. *Mental Health Journal,* 1974, *10* (4), 414-417.

Franks, C. M. *Behavior therapy: Appraisal and status.* New York: McGraw-Hill Book Co., 1969.

Friedman, P. H. The effects of modeling and role playing on assertive behavior. In R. D. Rubin, H. Fensterheim, A. A. Lazarus & C. M. Franks (Eds.), *Advances in behavior therapy.* New York: Academic Press, Inc., 1971.

Gambrill, E. D. & Richey, C. A. Personal communication, 1972.

Geisinger, D. L. Controlling sexual and interpersonal anxieties. In J. D. Krumboltz & C. E. Thoresen (Eds.), *Behavioral counseling: Cases and techniques.* New York: Holt, Rinehart and Winston, Inc., 1969.

Glasser, W. *Reality therapy.* New York: Harper & Row, 1965.

Goldfried, M. R. & Merbaum, M. (Eds.). *Behavior change through self-control.* New York: Holt, Rinehart and Winston, Inc., 1973.

Grimes, W., Moser, M. & Smith, C. *Assertion training.* La Mesa, CA: Grossmont Psychological Associates, 1975.

Guerra, J. J. The modification of stuttering behavior through response-contingent time out with the control of the subject's normal environmental stimuli. Unpublished doctoral dissertation, University of Nebraska, 1971.

Guerra, J. J. & Cotler, S. B. *Assertion training.* Sherman Oaks, CA: New Views Unlimited, 1975. (Audio cassette tapes)

Guerra, J. J. & Horsky, D. The use of "graduated" clients as role models in an assertion training group at a Free Clinic. Paper presented at Western Psychological Association, Anaheim, CA, April, 1973.

Hedquist, F. J. & Weinhold, B. K. Behavioral group counseling with socially anxious and unassertive college students. *Journal of Counseling Psychology,* 1970, *17,* 237-242.

Hersen, M., Eisler, R. M. & Miller, P. M. Development of assertive responses: Clinical, measurement, and research considerations. *Behaviour Research and Therapy,* 1973, *11,* 505-521.

Hersen, M., Eisler, R. M., Miller, P. M., Johnson, M. B. & Pinkston, S. G. Effects of practice, instructions and modeling on components of assertive behavior. *Behaviour Research and Therapy,* 1973, *11,* 443-453.

Homme, L., Csanyi, A. P., Gonzales, M. A. & Rechs, J. R. *How to use contingency contracting in the classroom.* Champaign, IL: Research Press Co., 1969.

Honig, W. K. *Operant behavior: Areas of research and application.* New York: Appleton-Century-Crofts, 1966.

Hosford, R. E. Overcoming fear of speaking in a group. In J. D. Krumboltz & C. E. Thoresen (Eds.), *Behavioral counseling: Cases and techniques.* New York: Holt, Rinehart and Winston, Inc., 1969.

Jacobs, B. Assertive training: A critical review. Research paper, George Peabody College for Teachers, 1974.

Jacobson, E. *Progressive relaxation.* Chicago: University of Chicago Press, 1938.

Jakubowski-Spector, P. Facilitating the growth of women through assertive training. *The Counseling Psychologist,* 1973, *4,* 75-87.

Jourard, S. M. *The transparent self* (rev. ed.). New York: D. Van Nostrand Company, 1971.

Kanfer, F. H. & Phillips, J. S. *Learning foundations of behavior therapy.* New York: John Wiley & Sons, Inc., 1970.

Kimble, G. A. *Hilgard and Marquis' conditioning and learning.* New York: Appleton-Century-Crofts, 1961.

Knox, D. *Marriage happiness: A behavioral approach to counseling.* Champaign, IL: Research Press Co., 1971.

Krumboltz, J. D. & Thoresen, C. E. *Behavioral counseling: Cases and techniques.* New York: Holt, Rinehart and Winston, Inc., 1969.

Lawrence, P. S. The assessment and modification of assertive behavior. Unpublished doctoral dissertation, Arizona State University, 1970.

Laws, D. R. & Serber, M. Measurement and evaluation of assertive training with sexual offenders. Paper presented at Association for Advancement of Behavior Therapy, Washington, D. C., 1971.

Lazarus, A. A. Behavior rehearsal vs. nondirective therapy vs. advice in effecting behavior change. *Behaviour Research and Therapy,* 1966, *4,* 209-212.

Lazarus, A. A. Behavior therapy in groups. In G. M. Gazda (Ed.), *Basic approaches to group psychotherapy and group counseling.* Springfield, IL: Charles C. Thomas, 1968.

Lazarus, A. A. *Behavior therapy and beyond.* New York: McGraw-Hill Book Co., 1971.

Lazarus, A. & Fay, A. *I can if I want to.* New York: William Morrow & Co., 1975.

Lesser, E. Behavior therapy with a narcotics user: A case report. *Behaviour Research and Therapy,* 1967, *5,* 251-252.

Liberman, R. Behavioral approaches to family and couple therapy. *American Journal of Orthopsychiatry,* 1970, *40,* 106-118.

Lomont, J. F., Gilner, F. H., Spector, N. J. & Skinner, I. K. Group assertive training and group insight therapies. *Psychological Reports*, 1969, *25*, 463-470.

Longin, H. E. & Rooney, W. M. Assertion training as a programmatic intervention for hospitalized mental patients. *Proceedings of the American Psychological Association*, Montreal, 1973, *8*, 459-560.

Mager, R. F. *Preparing instructional objectives*. Palo Alto, CA: Fearon Publishers, 1962.

McFall, R. M. & Lillesand, D. B. Behavior rehearsal with modeling and coaching in assertion training. *Journal of Abnormal Psychology*, 1971, *77*, 313-323.

McFall, R. M. & Marston, A. R. An experimental investigation of behavior rehearsal in assertive training. *Journal of Abnormal Psychology*, 1970, *76*, 295-303.

McFall, R. M. & Twentyman, C. T. Four experiments on the relative contributions of rehearsal, modeling, and coaching to assertion training. *Journal of Abnormal Psychology*, 1973, *11*, 199-218.

Melnick, J. A comparison of replication techniques in the modification of minimal dating behavior. *Journal of Abnormal Psychology*, 1973, *81*, 51-59.

Morrow, W. R. *Behavior therapy bibliography 1950-1969*. Columbia, MO: University of Missouri Press, 1971.

Neuman, D. Using assertive training. In J. D. Krumboltz & C. E. Thoresen (Eds.), *Behavioral counseling: Cases and techniques*. New York: Holt, Rinehart and Winston, Inc., 1969.

Newman, M. & Berkowitz, B. *How to be your own best friend*. New York: Ballantine Books, Inc., 1971.

O'Connor, R. D. Modification of social withdrawal through symbolic modeling. *Journal of Applied Behavior Analysis*, 1969, *2*, 15-22.

Otto, H. *More joy in your marriage*. New York: Hawthorn Books, Inc., 1969.

Paulson, T. L. The differential use of self-administered and group administered token reinforcement in group assertion training for college students. Unpublished doctoral dissertation, Fuller Theological Seminary, Pasadena, CA, 1974.

Piaget, G. W. & Lazarus, A. A. The use of rehearsal-desensitization. *Psychotherapy: Theory, Research, and Practice,* 1969, *6,* 264-266.

Phelps, S. & Austin, N. *The assertive woman.* San Luis Obispo, CA: Impact, 1975.

Rathus, S. A. An experimental investigation of assertive training in a group setting. *Journal of Behavior Therapy and Experimental Psychiatry,* 1972, *3,* 81-86.

Rathus, S. A. A 30-item schedule for assessing assertive behavior. *Behavior Therapy,* 1973a, *4,* 398-406.

Rathus, S. A. Instigation of assertive behavior through videotape-mediated assertive models and directed practice. *Behaviour Research and Therapy,* 1973b, *11,* 57-65.

Reynolds, G. S. *A primer of operant conditioning.* Atlanta, GA: Scott, Foresman and Co., 1968.

Ritter, B. The use of contact desensitization, demonstration plus participation and demonstration alone in the treatment of acrophobia. *Behaviour Research and Therapy,* 1969, *7,* 157-161.

Salter, A. *Conditioned reflex therapy.* New York: Creative Age Press, 1949.

Salter, A. Assertion training conversation session. Eighth annual convention of the Association for Advancement of Behavior Therapy, Chicago, 1974.

Shoemaker, M. E. & Paulson, T. L. Group assertion training for mothers as a family intervention in a child out-patient setting. Paper presented at the Western Psychological Association, Anaheim, CA, April, 1973.

Stampfl, T. G. & Levis, D. J. Essentials of implosive therapy: A learning-theory-based psychodynamic behavioral therapy. *Journal of Abnormal Psychology,* 1967, *72,* 496-503.

Stevens, J. *Awareness: Exploring, experimenting, experiencing.* Moab, UT: Real People Press, 1971.

Stevenson, I. & Wolpe, J. Recovery from sexual deviations through overcoming non-sexual neurotic responses. *American Journal of Psychiatry,* 1960, *116,* 737-742.

Stuart, R. B. Operant-interpersonal treatment for marital discord. *Journal of Consulting and Clinical Psychology,* 1969, *33,* 675-682.

Ullmann, L. & Krasner, L. *Case studies in behavior modification.* New York: Holt, Rinehart and Winston, Inc., 1965.

Vorenhorst, B. B. Helping a client speak up in class. In J. D. Krumboltz & C. E. Thoresen (Eds.), *Behavioral counseling: Cases and techniques.* New York: Holt, Rinehart and Winston, Inc., 1969.

Wagner, M. K. Reinforcement of the expression of anger through role-playing. *Behaviour Research and Therapy,* 1968, *6,* 91-95.

Weinman, B., Gelbart, P., Wallace, M. & Post, M. Inducing assertive behavior in chronic schizophrenics: A comparison of socioenvironmental, desensitization, and relaxation therapies. *Journal of Consulting and Clinical Psychology,* 1972, *39,* 246-252.

Willoughby, R. R. Norms for the Clark-Thurstone Inventory. *Journal of Social Psychology,* 1934, *5,* 91.

Wilson, A. E. & Smith, F. J. Counterconditioning therapy using free association: A case study. Paper presented at the American Psychological Association, 1968.

Wolpe, J. *Psychotherapy by reciprocal inhibition.* Stanford, CA: Stanford University Press, 1958.

Wolpe, J. *The practice of behavior therapy.* New York: Pergamon Press, Inc., 1969.

Wolpe, J. The instigation of assertive behavior: Transcripts from two cases. *Journal of Behavior Therapy and Experimental Psychiatry,* 1970, *1,* 145-151.

Wolpe, J. Supervision transcript: V—mainly about assertion training. *Journal of Behavior Therapy and Experimental Psychiatry,* 1973, *4,* 141-148.

Wolpe, J. & Lang, P. J. A fear survey schedule for use in behavior therapy. *Behaviour Research and Therapy,* 1964, *2,* 27.

Wolpe, J. & Lazarus, A. A. *Behavior therapy techniques: A guide to the treatment of neuroses.* New York: Pergamon Press, Inc., 1966.

Wolpe, J., Salter, A. & Reyna, L. J. *The conditioning therapies.* New York: Holt, Rinehart and Winston, Inc., 1966.

Young, E. R., Rimm, D. C. & Kennedy, T. D. An experimental investigation of modeling and verbal reinforcement in the modification of assertive behavior. *Behaviour Research and Therapy,* 1973, *11,* 317-319.